CCCC STUDIES IN WRITING & RHE
Edited by Steve Parks, University of Virginia

The aim of the CCCC Studies in Writing & Rhetoric (SWR) Series is to influence how we think about language in action and especially how writing gets taught at the college level. The methods of studies vary from the critical to historical to linguistic to ethnographic, and their authors draw on work in various fields that inform composition—including rhetoric, communication, education, discourse analysis, psychology, cultural studies, and literature. Their focuses are similarly diverse—ranging from individual writers and teachers, to work on classrooms and communities and curricula, to analyses of the social, political, and material contexts of writing and its teaching.

SWR was one of the first scholarly book series to focus on the teaching of writing. It was established in 1980 by the Conference on College Composition and Communication (CCCC) in order to promote research in the emerging field of writing studies. As our field has grown, the research sponsored by SWR has continued to articulate the commitment of CCCC to supporting the work of writing teachers as reflective practitioners and intellectuals.

We are eager to identify influential work in writing and rhetoric as it emerges. We thus ask authors to send us project proposals that clearly situate their work in the field and show how they aim to redirect our ongoing conversations about writing and its teaching. Proposals should include an overview of the project, a brief annotated table of contents, and a sample chapter. They should not exceed 10,000 words.

To submit a proposal, please register as an author at www.editorial manager.com/nctebp. Once registered, follow the steps to submit a proposal (be sure to choose SWR Book Proposal from the drop-down list of article submission types).

BLACK PERSPECTIVES IN WRITING PROGRAM ADMINISTRATION

FROM THE MARGINS TO THE CENTER

Edited by

Staci M. Perryman-Clark
Western Michigan University

and

Collin Lamont Craig
St. John's University

Conference on College
Composition and
Communication

National Council of
Teachers of English

Staff Editor: Bonny Graham
Manuscript Editor: Lee Erwin
Series Editor: Steve Parks
Interior Design: Mary Rohrer
Cover Design: Pat Mayer
Cover Image: Angelo Rodriguez

NCTE Stock Number: 03371; eStock Number: 03388
ISBN 978-0-8141-0337-1; eISBN 978-0-8141-0338-8

It is the policy of NCTE in its journals and other publications to provide a forum for the open discussion of ideas concerning the content and the teaching of English and the language arts. Publicity accorded to any particular point of view does not imply endorsement by the Executive Committee, the Board of Directors, or the membership at large, except in announcements of policy, where such endorsement is clearly specified.

NCTE provides equal employment opportunity (EEO) to all staff members and applicants for employment without regard to race, color, religion, sex, national origin, age, physical, mental or perceived handicap/disability, sexual orientation including gender identity or expression, ancestry, genetic information, marital status, military status, unfavorable discharge from military service, pregnancy, citizenship status, personal appearance, matriculation or political affiliation, or any other protected status under applicable federal, state, and local laws.

Every effort has been made to provide current URLs and email addresses, but because of the rapidly changing nature of the web, some sites and addresses may no longer be accessible.

Library of Congress Cataloging-in-Publication Data

Names: Perryman-Clark, Staci, editor. | Craig, Collin Lamont, 1979- editor.
Title: Black perspectives in writing program administration : from the margins to the center / edited by Staci M. Perryman-Clark and Collin Lamont Craig.
Description: Urbana, Illinois : National Council of Teachers of English, 2019. | Series: CCCC studies in writing & rhetoric | Includes bibliographical references and index.
Identifiers: LCCN 2019000312 (print) | LCCN 2019013577 (ebook) | ISBN 9780814103388 (ebook) | ISBN 9780814103371 (pbk) | ISBN 9780814103388 (e-ISBN)
Subjects: LCSH: Writing centers—Administration. | English language— Rhetoric—Study and teaching (Higher—Social aspects—United States. | African American college teachers—Attitudes.
Classification: LCC PE1404 (ebook) | LCC PE1404 .B5874 2019 (print) | DDC 808/.042071173—dc23
LC record available at https://lccn.loc.gov/2019000312

CONTENTS

FOREWORD: A FORENOTE FROM AN ANGRY BLACK MAN: BLACKNESS SHOULD ALWAYS BE CENTER

Vershawn Ashanti Young
University of Waterloo

OPENIN

Ahm a Angry Black Man
Ah say it loud
Wit plenty Style
B/c as James Baldwin say: ". . . to be a Negro in this country and to be relatively conscious, is to be in a rage almost all the time" (205). JB gotsta mean—for we in 20-upteen—that any *woke* black person is angry.
If dis true, then the other JB—that Godfather of Soul—might just as well had said: "Say it loud / I'm *angry* and I'm proud."

THE DIALOGUE

(this exchange tween me & JB previews Black Perspectives in Writing Program Administration, *a volume that includes insights on and from HBCUs, wit this very knowledge bespoke by WPAs from HBCUs! What's mo—tho this book is slammin in other ways too—is its progressive feminist focus and its attending specifying experiences of African American women.)*

Me (to the first JB): Check dis: ahm writin this foreword for *Black Perspectives in Writing Program Administration: From the Margins to the Center,* edited by my peeps, Staci Perryman-Clark and Collin Craig (also see they Chapter 5). Dis joint heah is *woke.* Got no choice but to be wid the likes of Carmen Kynard (Chapter 2) layin it down on the microaggressions that black WPA and black women specifically must endure—and do so to keep the black mind and body intact for dis heah work in writin instructin that she do. Then there's David F. Green Jr. (Chapter 3) puttin narratives of Afrocen-

vii

tric instruction up front for all. He say we can take a page from the rhetorical habitus of HBCUs. So wid all this going on, JB, how do readers and me too learn from this and express *woke* rage?

JB: You have to decide that you can't spend the rest of your life cursing out everybody who gets in your way.

Me: What?! We . . . ah . . . ah . . . ah can't?

JB: As a writer [academic, scholar, teacher, or insert role] you have to decide that what is really important is not that the people you write about [or teach] are Negroes, but that they are people, and that the suffering of any person is really universal.

Me: Word?! So, the focus of *woke* rage then is on the humanity of students/colleagues/people in the world/who suffer/who are black.

JB: If you can ever reach this level, if you can create a person [teach a person, understand a student] and make other people feel what this person feels, then it seems to me that you've gone much further, not only artistically [or academically], but socially, than in the ordinary, old-fashioned protest way.

SPITTIN KNOWLEDGE, YUP, THEORIZIN

Aiight, JB on point on how to be *woke*. Although me and him may differ a lil bit on the value of the "ordinary, old-fashioned protest way." Ah think protest important to any critical race progress; he think, at least in imaginative writing, that it overshadows the possibilities for empathy 'cross racial lines. He think this cuz in writin, the old protest way tend to blend blunt sociology into the literary human experience. At least dis what JB said Richard Wright's *Native Son* did in his review of that novel in "Everybody's Protest Novel."

This volume then on fleek cuz it straight presentin what ahm calling this blended *woke*ness—protest and humanity, racialized pedagogical experiences (Lockett et al.), and the possibilities for racial empathy (Wible in Chapter 4, and Inoue in Afterword).

So, let me get in where ah fit in on this blend then, and step to you wit two perspectives of my own. But fo ah offer my two protests, let me lay this on you bout black rage: As literary critic Addison Gayle says in his introduction to *The Black Aesthetic:* "The black artist in the American society who creates without interjecting a note of anger is creating not as a black man, but as an American. For anger in black art is as old as the first utterance by black men on American soil . . . " (xv–xvi). Gayle heah, on one hand, just sayin o'er what JB up top said before—to be conscious and black is to be constantly enraged. But on the other hand, he sayin something more: black anger is a fruitful framework for analysis and critique that can lead to needed changes. In this case it's both recognizing where blackness belongs in writin programs, writin instruction, and writin centers—upfront and center—and enactin dis perspective.

PROTEST 1: THE ROAD TO WRITIN STUDIES
IS PAVED WITH GOOD INTENTIONS

My friend and colleague Asao Inoue in the afterword to this volume say he self-consciously speakin to white WPAs cuz a lot of times they don't know how to listen across racial lines. (Ain't always dey fault tho. Society just don't teach em, require it of em. But we do.) But heah, let me speak self-consciously to or at least bout some black folk ah run cross on occasion—and far more than ah care to—black folk who ah hear say that there were some gooooood masters during slavery. Or, if they don't go that far, they say that there were some white masters who were good to those they enslaved / that they enslaved because it was the custom of the time / that despite owning other people, some gooood whites taught blacks to read, allowed them to marry, or did not sell em way from they family.

News flash, my people: these are things white folk should have been doing anyway—I mean, not selling other people may have been legal but it was still clearly wrong in 1619, 1719, and 1819; and segregation was wrong in 1919, 1929, 1939, 1949, and 1959; and slavery's and segregation's transmogrifications are and will still be wrong in 2019, 2029, and 2039. So gooood intentions is not an excuse, nor a pass, nor a tissue for neoliberal white folk tears—tears that flow when they told that black shoulda always been front and center in writin instruction—and keepin it off to da side . . . well, that's r_ _ _ _ _ .

Now why do I make this point to my black brethren—in an appeal, like David Walker? Cuz we got to decolonize our own minds, rinse that white supremacy right out. No black writin teacher—and no white one or Latinx one or Asian one either—should even tell their black students who use Black English, "you will never get a job / people will think that you ain't bright and whatnot." Cuz then you got to explain all those black millionaires and others makin a good livin, what we call a killin, using African American Language.

It should come as no surprise then that I am against code switching, replacing beautiful black speech and rhetoric with white ways with words. Nope. Ah adamantly disagree with this capitulation to code switching. Instead ah promote a line from the SRTOL background statement, that ask us to consider how "many of us have taught as though the function of schools and colleges were to erase differences." Then it asks this very important question: "would we accomplish more, both educationally and ethically, if we shifted [our] emphasis to precise, effective, and appropriate communication in diverse ways, whatever the dialect?"

This is a beautiful question. What would it look like if we stopped harping on dialect and focused on effective and appropriate communication? The problem is that too many can't reconcile what they consider to be academic discourse with "creativity and individuality."

To help explain why people can't reconcile effective communication with creativity, let me invoke a black writer, Toni Morrison (hear her anger).

In her essay, "Unspeakable Things Unspoken," Morrison writes:

> Looking at the scope of American literature, I can't help thinking that the question should never have been "Why am I, an Afro-American, absent from it?" . . . . The spectacularly interesting question is, "What intellectual feats had to be performed by the author or his critic to erase me from a society seething with my presence . . . ?"

One of the feats I routinely witness as I speak to teachers and tutors across the nation is this: teachers say that they recognize the importance of language diversity for students but they tell their students that they have to get ready for the teacher in the next class who will prejudge them or the employer who will not hire them— if they don't speak or write a certain way.

The feat here is that the teachers want to present themselves as antiracists, while at the same time they are the ones enacting the very prejudice on the student they say the student will experience outside.

In other words, the teacher is saying, I'm not racist, but I'm going to teach you in a way (how to switch off yo black) and grade in a way (that is down if you black in yo writin) that will prepare you to be acceptable to the folks who are really racist. The teacher then becomes the stand-in, the proxy, for the would-be racist. Now that's a feat: to contort oneself into being an antiracist and a surrogate-stand-in-racist at the same time; be both simultaneously a promoter of linguistic diversity and operate against it. Now this a feat that all writin programs and writin instructors, especially *woke* ones, must avoid.

PROTEST 2: YOU AIN'T GOD

Now dis heah protest, like Asao's, is self-consciously to my white peeps. "Recently after a talk I gave on a college campus about code meshing (y'all know ahm bout that blendin of styles and languages, bout Black Standard English), a white female teacher asked me how could she as a white teacher permit black students to use they language? I paused, slowed my response to a deliberate and careful pitch and said: You ain't God is you? God, s/he the one that give language and the capacity to use language. You, teacher, really don't have the authority to permit or restrict its use. That's a false orientation you got goin on. What Sartre call that? False consciousness? I said to her and say heah that this belief is one teachers got to abandon. (Whether you believe in God is not the point; the point is that language exceeds the bounds of what teachers should try to adjudicate, to have authority over.) As a teacher, and I encourage writin programs to take this up too, you can *support, join* students in learning to use all they language resources, all rhetorics available to them to good communicative effect. You provide resources for them, and they *bring* resources as well, and together they learn to develop agency and authenticity and authority over their own language use. Yo permission and yo restriction ain't ever part of the equation, making it so is the problem.

WHERE MY ALLIES AT?

Black folk and African American Language need allies if it gone enjoy its rightful place at the center of rhetorical and writin educa-tion. Yea, we need allies in writin programs, writin centers, and writing studies more broadly. And ahm talkin bout the for-real-puttin-they-neck-on-the-line allies, the kind that Omi Oshun Joni L. Jones describe in her speech "Six Rules for Allies." Now, Jones fo sho lettin the folks have it when she clarify that allies (1) "know that it is not sufficient to be liberal. In fact, the liberal position is ac-tually a walk backwards . . . The liberal position supports the status quo of the academy which means that racism, sexism, homopho-bia, the perils of nationhood, and a commitment to class structures cannot be undone in the academy—unless we move toward a radi-cal rather than a liberal position." She say that real allies must (2) "Be loud and crazy so Black folks won't have to be! Speak up! Say it! Name it!" She say to allies: (3) "Do not tell anyone in any op-pressed group to be patient," and that they (4) must "recognize the new racism, the new sexism, the old homophobia. It is institutional and structural." She encourages allies not to be skittish: (5) "When called out about your racism, sexism, or homophobia, don't cower in embarrassment, don't cry, and don't silently think 'she's crazy' and vow never to interact with her again. We are all plagued by racism, sexism, and homophobia. Be grateful that someone took the time to expose yours—remember, exposure allows the wind to whip away isolation and fear." And last she say, (6) "Allies actively support alternative possibilities." They support student agency.

Agency—this is something ah tell my students that they all must continue to develop. Agency, ah tell them, is they capacity to write, yes perform, in the ways that emanate from the combination of they attitudes, languages, beliefs, inclinations, philosophies, and motivations and rhetorics. Ah urge them to recognize and accept their own agency, which means despite any and all advice and instruction they may be given, they must always ask: Now that ah've heard this and seen that, what does my mind and soul tell me to do? How now must ah speak and write? Then they should push that. So my ending word on this fore-note is this: Writin program administrators, instructors, advisors, tutors, directors, and others must also learn to get out of the way of black students' agency and learn to allow, support, and help steer it.

CLOSIN

Yea, Ahm a angry black man
I say it loud
In my style
B/c as James Baldwin say: " . . . to be a Negro in this country and to be relatively conscious, is to be in a rage almost all the time" ("Negro" 205).

JB got to mean—for we in 20-upteen—that any *woke* black person gots to be angry at the way s/he taught to write, with the common deficiency perspectives abounding, the lack of appreciation for and willful ignorance of African American Language, and how writin is missin all that black rhetorical prowess up in schools.

Staci and Collin and Carmen and David and Scott and Alexandria and Shawanda and Brian and Adrienne and Jonathan and Jeanne and Asao tappin on they tom-tom tryin to get us *woke* folk to *act* on this black perspective: Put blackness in writin instruction and writin programs up front and center.

WORKS CITED

Baldwin, James. "Everybody's Protest Novel." *Partisan Review,* vol. 16, no. 6, June 1949, pp. 578–85; reprinted in *Notes of a Native Son,* by Baldwin, Beacon Press, 1955, pp. 13–23.

Baldwin, James, Emile Capouya, Lorraine Hansberry, Nat Hentoff, Langston Hughes, and Alfred Kazin. "The Negro in American Culture: A Symposium." *CrossCurrents,* vol. 11, no. 3, Summer 1961, pp. 205–24.

Gayle, Addison, Jr., ed. *The Black Aesthetic.* Doubleday, 1971.

Jones, Omi Oshun Joni L. "Six Rules for Allies." Video talk, vimeo. com/78945479.

Morrison, Toni. "Unspeakable Things Unspoken: The Afro-American Presence in American Literature." Lecture delivered at the University of Michigan, 7 Oct. 1988; published in *Michigan Quarterly Review,* vol. 28, no. 1, Winter 1989, pp. 1–34.

Students' Right to Their Own Language [SRTOL]. National Council of Teachers of English and Conference on College Composition and Communication, 1974, 2014, http://cccc.ncte.org/cccc/ resources/positions/srtolsummary.

1

Introduction: Black Matters: Writing Program Administration in Twenty-First-Century Higher Education

Staci M. Perryman-Clark and Collin Lamont Craig

> Nearly a century later we confine discussions about race in America to the "problems" black people pose for whites rather than consider what this way of viewing people reveals about us as a Nation.
>
> —Cornel West, *Race Matters*

THE STUDY OF RACE, INCLUDING ITS INTELLECTUAL, theoretical, and methodological aspects, continues to be a hot topic of scholastic inquiry; and the field of rhetoric and composition is no exception. More recently, conversations concerning race have been discussed in writing program administration (WPA) scholarship. These conversations have highlighted how making race visible in our intersecting administrative and curricular practices creates opportunities to both explore and problematize writing program administration as a framework for institutional and disciplinary critique. In 2011, we published "Troubling the Boundaries: (De)Constructing WPA Identities at the Intersections of Race and Gender," where we called into question the limited representation of faculties and scholars of color in the Council of Writing Program Administrators (CWPA) conferences. Upon the publication of "Troubling the Boundaries," CWPA as an organization requested feedback from us on how CWPA could be more inclusive. From that conversation, CWPA established a mentoring project to support new WPAs and WPAs of color. As part of the mentoring project, various scholars contributed blog posts responding to some of the issues we addressed in "Troubling the Boundaries." While we found these early conversations to be quite productive, we knew that CWPA and larger organizations like CCCC would need to embark on calls to action that moved beyond dialogue. We knew that there needed to be a breadth of practical takeaway strategies that could address the complexities of structural racism and enact real change that mattered.

As scholars who engage race in WPA work, we are pleased to see calls to action that engage race and WPA research in scholarship. We are pleased to see the "Symposium: Challenging Whiteness and/in Writing Program Administration and Writing Programs" published in the Spring 2016 *WPA: Writing Program Administration*. In this special issue, the editors frame conversations about race in relation to the "[v]iolence in Ferguson and DC; the creation of #blacklivesmatter; the killings of Trayvon Martin, Tamir Rice, Ramarley Graham, Freddie Gray, Sean Bell, Jonathan Ferrell, Darius Simmons, Ernest Hoskins and Oscar Grant; the deaths of Sandra Bland, Kindra Chapman, Joyce Curnell, Ralkina Jones and Raynette Turner . . . " (1). We also acknowledge the timeliness of this publication. Not long after its appearance in print, two more Black men, Alton Sterling and Philando Castile, were gunned down by police. In fact, the news of Castile's killing appeared in the media at the very moment when we were drafting this book chapter! Given these current events, there couldn't be a more kairotic moment to consider how they inform the rhetorical situation of blackness in twenty-first-century higher education.

For us, the work published in "Troubling the Boundaries" and *WPA*'s "Fall 2016 Symposium" very much shape how we understand the racial macro- and microaggressions we experienced as WPAs and faculty of color. While we've shared snippets of our experiences in both our first collaborative article, "Troubling the Boundaries," and our follow-up article in the "Fall 2016 Symposium," "Troubling the Boundaries Revisited," we quickly recognized that we did not have enough space to thoroughly tease out the implications for both allies and WPAs of color who administer writing programs. It was during the revision stages of "Troubling the Boundaries Revisited" that we discovered that this work needed a more extensive book project, and so we began brainstorming what such a project might look like.

For us, such a project needs to include additional experiences with racism, navigating institutional constraints, and the challenges to cultivating and sustaining administrative agency that WPAs of color face. We've shared a few experiences in our previous publications, but there is much more to tell. For instance, when reflecting on previous publications, Staci needed to omit an experience about being denied summer compensation for WPA work, while a white male colleague in her department self-reported guaranteed summer teaching and a summer stipend for advising undergraduate students over the summer. When Staci confronted administrative leadership, she was told that no one received summer compensation, despite her colleague's self-reporting, only to later be told by another administrator that the colleague was indeed compensated. For her, race and gender equity intersect, and the implications for exploring that inequity alone warranted another article or chapter. While race and gender intersect in much of Staci's experiences, the racial implications associated with WPAs of color cannot simply be ignored. Staci needed more than another "model of anti-oppressive and anti-racist . . . work [that] question[s] power relationships in society in producing and reproducing racial and gendered sources of oppression" (Graham 424). While it is useful to consider antioppressive and antiracist work in relation to racial and gender hegemony, such work often subscribes to "a Eurocentric[ity] that fails to understand, recognise or respond to black autonomy" (424). For Staci, this meant considering the precise role of blackness as its own cultural epistemological framework that informs the work she does as WPA in her writing program.

With other experiences, Staci, as the only black woman on specific committees, found herself having to argue continuously for diversity and access for students when embarking on curricular reform efforts including graduate curriculum reform and general education. In both cases, resistance to these efforts did not come from white men alone, but also, and more often, from white women who could readily champion gender equity, but remained obstinate—or, at best, silent—when Staci raised concerns that applied to students of color. When working on general education curricular reform, while Staci made the case for diversity and inclusion learning outcomes to be embedded in every distribution area, members of the committee, all white and cis-gendered, quickly dismissed her pleas because they found them to be too prescriptive and not feasible for programmatic assessment. As a compromise, because there were no additional allies in the room to support her proposals, Staci had to accept that diversity and inclusion learning outcomes would be those addressed in skills-based courses across disciplines. In other instances on this committee, Staci's credentials would be questioned by white male colleagues when making the case for first-year writing courses to be taught by trained faculty instructors. Referring to CCCC's "Principles for the Postsecondary Teaching of Writing," a "go-to" document for WPAs, did her no good. The irony of this experience was that no other colleagues' disciplinary knowledge or credentials were questioned. While one might concede that the mythic notion that anyone could teach writing (Kahn) poses a challenge for any WPA, regardless of subjectivity, the same colleague questioning Staci's credentials further stated that Staci needed checks and balances, a charge that was not made toward any other colleagues on the committee. Such an assumption suggests a conformity to whiteness's status of power, authority, and generation of knowledge when blackness is positioned as a threat to white supremacy as an institutional construct.

During another meeting, on graduate curriculum reform in her English department, debate occurred when colleagues in literary studies argued against a curricular reform that would remove distribution requirements for studying knowledge by literary time period. One particular colleague, white and female, questioned how a student could complete a PhD in English without studying literary periods before the 1600s, periods that have historically and traditionally omitted the experiences of people of color. As a result of this discussion, Staci boldly proclaimed that the current curriculum in use was one of the whitest curricula she had seen: She reminded colleagues that those trained in many rhetoric and writing programs often do not take coursework in literary periods, yet are qualified to teach rhetoric and writing courses offered in English departments. She also reminded her colleagues that not all knowledge, especially knowledge generated from Afrocentric study, is investigated chronologically. After a few colleagues were unwilling to abandon literary study by historical periods, Staci boldly asked, "If we really want to think about chronology, why don't we go all the way back to Africa, the cradle of civilization?" Gasps emerged from colleagues, especially white women. #micdrop!

For Staci, these experiences illustrate racial microaggressions and resistance both from those who shared her gender identity and from those who did not. In our previous two articles, "Troubling the Boundaries," and "Troubling the Boundaries Revisited," we address the intersecting identities between race and gender; however, as we have continued reflecting and doing intellectual work, we have also continued to understand specific racial microaggressions associated with our being black that challenge our roles as WPAs and colleagues doing curricular work. Staci has since written about her experiences as a WPA responding to resistance not only from GTAs to her authority, but also from colleagues to the GTAs' commitment and desire to work on behalf of students of color ("Who We Are[n't] Assessing"; "Creating a United Front"; "Race, Teaching Assistants, and Student Bullying"). While implications of gender are explored, each of these works examines more critically the implications of those teaching, assessing, and making judgments about what students of color can and cannot do; she has also written about experiences that specifically affect black students who have been referred for intensive first-year writing remediation. Thus we felt a critical need for scholarship that addresses microaggressions for both faculty and WPAs of color and students of color, and furthermore establishes a firm commitment to examine the relationships between our being African American, African American students in higher education, and the current sociopolitical landscape for African Americans in a twenty-first-century context.

After Collin's first year as a writing professor on the tenure track, his WPA left to take a job elsewhere. The rumor mill of unchecked racial microaggressions from colleagues and volatile working conditions echoed in the whispers of faculty-lounge gossip regarding the cause of her swift exit. While any new junior faculty member of color might find this troubling, Collin knew that program politics in WPA work were an inevitable part of the job. And so his pretenure mantra was: Be collegial, find allies, teach your classes well, and write. In the following year, the Vice Provost for Undergraduate Education and Director of Core Studies was assigned as the interim WPA, and the full-time writing faculty divided much of the administrative duties of the program. Collin and his colleagues visited one another's classes, led summer teaching retreats, approved program syllabi for graduate students, and sat on committees that hired contingent faculty. He collaborated with other junior faculty to revise the program learning objectives, volunteered to mentor TAs and part-time writing faculty, and partnered with colleagues to coordinate their annual end-of-year student writing conference. The work of the WPA organically took on a collective identity of faculty in the program. By the spring semester, Collin was also co-coordinating a high school bridge program, a structured mentoring project that partnered high school students with writing professors. He had also recently published in a prominent journal in writing studies and was finally getting his research off the ground. In spite of the recent department drama, he wanted to demonstrate his work ethic and commitment to excelling in his first tenure-track job.

Midsemester, the interim WPA sent an email stating that he wanted to speak with Collin about his progress. Given everything Collin was doing, he welcomed the opportunity. The following day the WPA visited Collin's office. The exchange went something like this: "So how are things?" the WPA asked. Collin thought to invite him to sit. But this was looking to be a quick chat. He spoke about some of the administrative work he was doing for the program. Feeling inspired that he had found a sense of belonging in his new position and was actively contributing, he mentioned his work to revise the program learning objectives, and remarked on the success and high student participation of the recent annual student writing conference, an event that he volunteered to help organize in coming years. "That's good," the WPA responded, still standing in the doorway, arms folded and with a tone that seemed to contradict what was meant to be an affirmation, "but you should give other faculty a chance to coordinate the event." His nonchalant dismissal was quick and indicative that this was not going to be a congratulatory visit.

In a strange line of questioning that followed, the WPA would go on to ask why Collin was missing faculty meetings. Collin reminded him of the research project he was launching. He reminded the WPA of their previous discussions about how it would conflict with the monthly faculty meeting schedule. Before taking on this project, he sought department and university approval because of this time conflict. He reminded the interim WPA of this granted approval to miss meetings, an approval that he had secured from the dean, and clarified his commitment to service responsibilities, just for good measure. But none of this seemed to pacify his director or sway what now seemed like an intent to put Collin in his place. His WPA then suggested that there were some "inconsistencies" on Collin's curriculum vitae that he recently included as a supporting document with the annual faculty report to the university, an accusation that turned out to be false, and a document the WPA could only have accessed using unethical measures. "You should be careful when getting those documents together," he said in warning. "You should let me help you next time." These interrogations were rapid and infantilizing. But more critically, they implied that not only was Collin not fulfilling his responsibilities as a faculty member but that his academic integrity was also in question.

As this WPA stood halfway in Collin's office, dealing out one criticism after another, his whiteness had eventually become apparent. It was a moment where Collin's simmering racial paranoia had faced a prophetic truth that one day he would no longer be safe in spite of all of his efforts and mantras to maintain safety. You see, Collin had crafted a manicured version of his black self for these kinds of situations. This curated self: careful and readymade to diffuse any existential dangers when interacting with white folks in positions of power. It is the portable identity that one takes to conferences and to campus-wide teaching workshops and university-wide committees where we are leveraged by the university for our de facto diversity perspective. It is your psychic armor when you know that showing out or "keepin' it real" won't keep yo' black self a job at a predominately white institution. Collin had mentally rehearsed these kinds of interactions over and over when he prepared for campus job talks. He knew the unbreakable smile he would give to the racially insensitive question. He knew the defusing words he would offer in response to the microaggression hurled at him that masqueraded as intellectual curiosity about his research during Q&A sessions. These are African American vernacular strategies of survival that are grounded in black epistemologies; they are "ways that African Americans come to know and act in response to their environments" (Richardson 34–35). They are taxonomies of verbal and nonverbal practices by which black folk achieve agency, or, put another way, how we make a way outta no way; or, put another way, strategic interjections into the ivory tower so that we can survive and do our work.

Collin recollected the stories he had read of black folk who had come to realize when subject position meant everything as they navigated their departments and disciplines. Jacqueline Jones Royster calls these the moments "when we are compelled to respond to a rendering of our potential that demands, not that we account for attitudes, actions, and conditions, but that we defend ourselves as human beings" (31). But even more, they are moments when subject position teaches those living in vulnerable bodies about abjection and surveillance. These moments are the complementary folklore to the clichéd narrative of black suffering. Collin despised this narrative for the prophetic truth that it always told. And now, while sharing his office with what he had realized to be a bullying white male writing program director, he had become the cliché (Als 137). Were there other black faculty whom he had spoken to this way? Other pretenured arrogant Negroes who had gotten out of line and needed a quick serving of managerial correction? There usually are. These interactions are rhetorical in how they produce a kind of tragic black existential reality. It is a reality that illuminates how white male administrative subjectivity as a regulative project of institutional whiteness reifies the status of the black subject as subalterned. More broadly, it is a reality that illuminates how institutional whiteness legislates the conditions of legibility and positionality for black bodies, black labor, and black intellectual work in a university writing program.

Understood through an African American rhetorical framework, this WPA's line of interrogation of Collin's work progress and academic credentials meant that on any given day his job and, by extension, his world could be drastically altered by how this WPA chose to see him. And this man's subject position as white male administrator at a predominately white institution made it so. The audacity and prevailing norm of white men as administrators that served as the backdrop at our Catholic institution made it so. When whiteness exists as the institutional and administrative norm it also functions as a floating signifier that regulates disciplinary and department discourses and permits these kinds of bullying to go unchecked. And as a consequence of this norm, gendered administrative whiteness is always and already centered as precursory to any racial paranoia black faculty may experience: the paranoia of being watched, losing one's job, having one's credentials scrutinized, or being subjugated to a range of interrogations and unchecked microaggressions. Collin imagined the swift exit of that black sista WPA after his first year on the tenure track. He wondered if she had performed a readymade version of her black self before she decided to pack up and leave.

There are some meaningful conclusions one might draw from this interaction. At best, it demonstrated an occasion for how we might use African American centered frameworks to interpret and theorize ways that race matters in our relations with institutional administrators. It reveals that WPA discourse, as an amalgamation of experiences, bodies, labor, policies, rules, departments, and documents, is always and already race work. And for black faculty engaging with WPA work, there are a myriad of categories that we must factor into this labor. As editors of this collection, we have realized a few: Comporting blackness to minimize white anxiety is race work. Deciding how one chooses to be visible on campus is race work. Deciding whether or not to apply for positions after combing department websites looking for black faculty is race work. What we decide to teach is race work. How we dress is race work. Achieving legibility in front of panoptic white administrative gazes is race work. Coddling white fragility is race work. Our decision to smile or not in weekly faculty meetings is race work. How we respond to microaggressions is race work. How we empathize with white liberal guilt is race work. How we succeed and fail as administrators is race work. And born out of our efforts to perform this labor are the dissonances that come with the daily struggles of having to choose: Between leaving and staying at our jobs to support the faculty and graduate students of color that lean on us for support, mentoring, and the courses that we teach. Between the lie of diversity initiatives and the truth of gatekeeping hiring and curricular practices. Between black silence and white faculty murmurings as to why we never come to department parties or retreats. Between talking too little and talking too much.

These realities have greater consequences as we experience an unprecedented historical moment in our public discourse where political campaigns are won on xenophobic rhetoric, draconian measures to regulate our Muslim communities, and presidential talking points that equate the agendas of white supremacists and those of social justice activists—all practices that demonstrate a commitment to reaffirming racist power asymmetries that work to regulate vulnerable bodies of color. We are in a moment in which racism and racist logics are no longer sanitized in coded language or veiled by political rhetoric. And we must ask how these rhetorical projects bleed into our institutional practices, are coded into our administrative agendas, and are reflected in our programmatic objectives and interpersonal relations. When white heterosexual men misuse their administrative power while living in bodies that are always already raced and gendered citations of historically and politically maintained power asymmetries endemic of the ivory tower, we must ask how race and racism are circulating in our writing programs. We must consider how the policing of black bodies, black labor, and black intellectual work in our writing programs functions as citations of larger political projects to disenfranchise historically vulnerable and marginalized groups. Centering WPA discourse as intersectional critical race work is an opportunity for exploring these subjects of inquiry as critical interventions. It positions us to cultivate antiracist responses from the perspective of those of color (not simply as Eurocentric appropriations), and enact socially responsible approaches to program building. It positions us to build allies and create rhetorical situations for students and faculty to imagine rhetorics that speak truth to oppressive and divisive ideologies within and beyond the ivory tower, and more specifically within our writing programs.

Thus, we begin our call by responding to Staci's call to her colleagues that we "go all the way back to Africa." For us, Africa is a metaphor for locating the root of black thought in US writing programs, one that enables us to thoroughly explore an evolution of racism, microaggressions, and success in twenty-first-century higher education. In response to the additional microaggressive experiences we share here, we approach this book with the hope that we might move from sharing of microaggressions toward sharing of successes by black WPAs and WPAs whose work represents a strong commitment to students of color, and, in our case, black students; and toward fostering stronger alliance building among white allies in our field. It is through this progression of rhetorical moves that we not only seek to better understand our own work and its implications for black WPAs and WPAs of color, but also and more important that we have concrete and specific models for taking action to confront and resist racist microaggressions. For us, the shift from racialized experiences toward alliance building and allyship comes at a critical, historical moment, where the lives and embodiments of black perspectives in higher education must be carefully examined.

WHY BLACKNESS MATTERS: WHY NOW

As editors of this collection, we also wish to emphasize the timeliness of moving from broader studies of whiteness and race to the study of blackness in relation to WPA work in higher education. One of the reasons we advocate this shift to blackness as part of the narrative and research we do with race in higher education is the shifting population of students who enroll in our postsecondary institutions, and, in effect, in our campus writing programs. Given the current landscape in the United States, black women are one of the fastest-growing groups enrolling in postsecondary programs. A 2014 study confirmed that black women currently lead all racial and gender groups when it comes to higher education enrollment (Danielle par. 2). Another study confirmed: "For the first time in the history of data collection by the National Center of Education Statistics as reported by the US Census, Black women have surpassed every other group in this country based upon race and gender" ("Black Women" par. 1). In addition, Howard Professor Ivory Toldson has found a "sharp spike in college enrollment among Black men" ("Nine Biggest Lies about Black Males"). In contrast, a more recent *Forbes* study revealed that college enrollment among white males has been on a consistent decline (CCAP). In short, given the fact that racial demographics are changing in higher education, the shape of such conversations on race must also shift. We see a focus on blackness in WPA work as one of many opportunities to address these shifting demographics.

In the wake of xenophobic rhetoric in politics, trends of police brutality, and the reawakening of public discourse on race, current and historical events surrounding the state of blackness in the United States also require us to pay close attention to the relationship between these events and the work we do within our institutions. In this chapter, we previously cited the *WPA: Writing Program Administration* editors' references to current events related to the violence in Ferguson and Washington, DC. The editors write:

> The violence in Ferguson and DC; the creation of #blacklivesmatter; the killings of Trayvon Martin, Tamir Rice, Ramarley Graham, Freddie Gray, Sean Bell, Jonathan Ferrell, Darius

Simmons, Ernest Hoskins and Oscar Grant; the deaths of
Sandra Bland, Kindra Chapman, Joyce Curnell, Ralkina
Jones and Raynette Turner while in police custody brought
national attention to the realities of majority minority citizens
in this country. We call out these names to remind us that
many of us are able to turn our heads and close the doors, as
our privilege allows, to these injustices. All too often we forget
the names of these individuals because our communities, our
cultures, our families, and our homes are not subject to the
violence of racial intolerance. (1)

Current events surrounding violence in relation to black citizens
in the United States have hit even closer to home. In 2014, both
NCTE and CCCC condemned the violence and police brutality
inflicted on one of our own CCCC members and long-time members of the NCTE/CCCC Black Caucus, Ersula Ore, an assistant
professor at Arizona State University. Their letter to Arizona State
University Provost Page and President Crow, signed by past NCTE
President Ernest Morrell and CCCC chair Adam Banks states:

If there is any institution we should be able to count on to
advance the ideal that all people are equal, that all people
should feel safe in the pursuit of learning, it is the university.
However, the treatment of Dr. Ore by university police, vo-
ciferously supported by President Crow's statement of support, undermines our confidence in Arizona State University's commitment to basic equality and leaves us questioning
whether ASU is in any way serious about its often expressed
commitments to diversity. (par. 1)

While the letter does not directly mention blackness or black bodies, it is important to emphasize this racial profiling and police brutality inflicted on Dr. Ore, a black female body, which functions as
a system of police brutality and state sanctioned violence inflicted
upon black male and female bodies. It also goes without notice that
this letter was signed by past NCTE and CCCC leaders, both of
whom represent the presence of black bodies in higher education
and disciplinary organizations.

In addition to NCTE and CCCC's statement in support of Dr. Ore, the NCTE/CCCC Black Caucus also published a statement affirming #blacklivesmatter in 2015. In the first paragraphs of this statement, leaders of the Black Caucus acknowledge the timeliness and necessity for literacy and writing educators to affirm #black-livesmatter in their call to action: "At this pivotal moment, between a space of hopeful resistance and fragile defiance, the dilemmas of race and racism in the United States have become so copious that to ignore them would be to render NCTE voiceless and bequeath it to those great chasms of silence through which racial injustices endure" (par. 1). What is also important to note is that this statement specifically signals blackness and schooling in relation to the criminal justice system in the United States:

> The picture of US racism begins with our children (though it does not end with them). While they comprise 18 percent of the preschool population, Black children represent over 50 percent of all out-of-preschool suspensions. A recent analysis by researchers at Villanova University concluded that in addition to racial bias, Black girls face colorism: darker skin tone significantly raised Black girls' odds of being put out of school. To this point, we now know that Black girls are six times more likely to be suspended than White girls, just as Black boys are imprisoned at six times the rate of their White counterparts. Moreover, Black children are 18 times more likely to be sentenced as adults than White children, and make up nearly 60 percent of children in prison. While we could cite hundreds of comparable statistics, the evidence is unambiguous—racial inequities in the US prevail from the cradle to the grave. (par. 3)

For us, the final paragraph of the NCTE statement affirming #blacklivesmatter sums up the reason we choose to emphasize the relationship between blackness and the work we do in higher education: Because black lives do matter and the time is now for organizations including NCTE, CCCC, and CWPA to work together to affirm black lives as they promote racial equality and eliminate injustice within and beyond our organizations and institutions of higher education:

> Recognition of structures of racial hatred sits at the center of our conviction as an organization. This statement seeks to affirm what should be obvious: Black lives matter. As an educational organization committed to equity and educational justice, promoting literacy and human life, we take seriously our obligation to ensure racial justice. Therefore, we remain resolute in our mission to use and produce knowledge that is essential to eliminating racism in the US and beyond. (par. 8)

As one example of this affirmation, we offer the CCCC 2016 revised Statement on Ebonics, where the relationships among black identity, language, and lives are firmly established and recognized. In their revised version of this statement, authors from the CCCC Language Policy Committee write: "Ebonics reflects the Black experience and conveys Black traditions and socially real truths. Black Languages are crucial to Black identity. Black Language sayings, such as 'What goes around comes around,' are crucial to Black ways of being in the world. Black Languages, like Black lives, matter" (par. 13). We couldn't agree more; engaging blackness and its implications for the work we do in campus writing programs occurs at a precise kairotic moment that counters the assault on black lives and black intellectualism in the United States.

Additionally, we acknowledge and affirm larger-scale projects in relation to how we see and understand the importance of black lives in our discipline. However, we also recognize that more work needs to be done at specific, yet varying, locations and institutional sites. What is also missing from much of this previous disciplinary work is the ways in which individual and racialized narratives affect issues in writing program administration differently. In essence, we believe that the discipline must now direct its attention beyond macrodisciplinary experiences, as we venture into the weeds in search for experiences and narratives that are less familiar to readers, narratives that position black experiences more directly in relation to WPA work. Thus, we seek to share those experiences that are less commonly familiar.

In relation to the role of black lives in higher education, we further assert that the time is now to signal attention directly to higher education, with organizations such as NCTE, CCCC, and CWPA serving as guides, for what we want literacy and writing education to look like in twenty-first-century higher education. Organizations such as these can provide leading voices on the value of black lives, black language, and African-centered practices in campus writing programs. However, it is also critical to acknowledge the limited scope of attention to African-centered practices in WPA scholarship. While Collin and I have previously argued that "within the field of composition and rhetoric, identity politics as a trope has been central when charting the terrain of discourse power relations between dominant and minority representations" ("Troubling" 40), African Americans have made specific—yet often untapped—contributions to WPA work. In addition to the works offered in both "Troubling the Boundaries" and "Troubling the Boundaries Revisited," Barbara L'Eplattenier and Lisa Mastrangelo's collection, *Historical Studies of Writing Program Administration Individuals, Communities, and the Formation of a Discipline*, does highlight a couple of contributions from African Americans. Of the HBCU writing program experience, while Deany Cheramie writes that HBCUs were committed to educating African American students during the early twentieth century, she also contends that an HBCUs like Xavier University in Louisiana, which she profiles, was "not capable of supporting a writing program administrator during the first five decades of its existence" (146). Moreover, while Cheramie describes the complicated history of this support as grounded within a historical and geopolitical climate designed around racism, narratives such as these position HBCU writing programs from the perspective of deficit in their ability to offer support and therefore contribute significantly to WPA narratives and histories of the field. In fact, as Sherri Craig has also observed of Cheramie's account, "An historical examination of the HBCU Xavier University of Louisiana by Deany Cheramie reveals no evidence of a person of color administering the program in the first fifty years of the university's existence" (17). Therefore, the black perspective as it relates to WPA leadership is excluded from this account.

Collie Fulford's discussion of HBCUs in her essay "Hit the Ground Listening: An Ethnographic Approach to New WPA Learning" similarly identifies challenges and assumptions about HBCU support for writing programs. In that essay, she describes her experiences of trying to make too-abrupt changes while directing an HBCU writing program as a new WPA, explaining that she had not read previous studies of white WPAs at HBCUs who had also tried to make changes too abruptly (161). While Fulford attributes her understandings of ethnographic research to her ability to learn from HBCU faculty when contributing to and revising a writing program, her discussion centers more on what she learned from ethnographic methods than it does on her position as a white body navigating and making decisions about how her policies and practices represent black perspectives and bodies.

Craig has called attention to the absence of both African American and HBCU experiences in WPA narratives not only with her critique of Cheramie's recollection of WPA work at Xavier University, but also of the exclusion of WPA narratives more broadly. She writes:

> To address this false assumption of ownership, writing program administration scholarship and the CWPA organization must collect more narratives that link the individual experience of WPAs of color to the social collective and internal conversations that help validate the long-established use of storytelling in defining and decoding WPA work. Overall, the absence of people of color in the field's common histories, whether intentional or not, silently and systematically reaffirms the marginality of non white, unprivileged narratives. (17)

Of black perspectives, Craig further expresses the need for the field to understand the ways in which young black professionals like her share their own stories in relation to WPA work. With reference to Jacqueline Jones Royster and Jean C. Williams's essay, "History in the Spaces Left," she demands that the field "resist dominant narratives by offering a fully developed discussion of Blacks in composition studies," while also "counter[ing] mythologies" about the experiences of blackness shared in WPA scholarship. In order to counter mythologies, Craig asserts a need for (1) acknowledging the fact that the presence of blackness in WPA scholarship is "typically disregarded," and that (2) including the black experience changes the history of rhetoric and composition (18). In short, providing an accurate account and history of WPA work and rhetoric and composition requires that the field include the histories and perspectives of people of African descent in its account of WPA work.

As for us, we seek to find those experiences that focus primarily on black people as racialized bodies in relation to writing program administration scholarship, scholarship that is less frequently explored in comparison to other narratives and perspectives on blackness in writing studies. As a result, we propose to position blackness and black bodies as a focus in the work that teachers and scholars do in writing program administration at specific sites and campus locations. We aim to frame the black body as both a political and a theoretical project. In doing so, we move from the obscuring of such narratives toward more visible opportunities for inclusion in composition. Additionally, we seek to situate the black perspective as intersectional and as providing a nuanced exploration of writing program administration that brings the unique experiences of black faculty, students, scholarship, and administrative work from margin to center. While it is distinct from conversations on race more broadly, we situate our focus on blackness as part of the tradition of research and scholarship surrounding race in higher education. In other words, we offer a focus on blackness as one part of the racial narrative of scholarship in WPA work. Blackness offers an illuminating part of the racial narrative that seeks to unblur conflations of race, whiteness, and privilege by affirming and acknowledging the intricacies that surround the work of black bodies and students who work within our postsecondary writing programs.

SHIFTING TO SPECIFIC LOCATIONS FOR BLACKNESS IN WRITING PROGRAM ADMINISTRATION: AN AFROCENTRIC APPROACH

We believe that an Afrocentric approach to understanding the shift from macro-approaches to black contributions and intellectual work in disciplinary statements toward more concrete experiences at specific institutional sites is necessary. Therefore, we position an Afrocentric theoretical framework as a focus for understanding the work of black WPAs, the impacts of WPA work on black lives, and the fostering of alliances across institutional and disciplinary contexts. When defining Afrocentric theories of education, Jacqueline Jordan Irvine writes that most scholars "agree that an Afrocentric curriculum [includes] a systematic study of the multidimensional aspects of black thought and practice centered around the contributions and heritage of people of African descent" ("Afrocentric Education" 201). In *Afrocentric Teacher-Research: Rethinking Appropriateness and Inclusion*, Staci M. Perryman-Clark further argues that Afrocentric education is "grounded in worldviews employing educational practices that are culturally situated within the interests of the people of the African Diaspora, regardless of institutional or organizational infrastructures" (9). With reference to the ways in which the African worldview has been taken up in rhetoric and composition scholarship, Elaine Richardson clarifies that such a worldview refers to "the knowledge that Black folks have about how to negotiate Blackness in everyday situations" (*African American Literacies* 27).

It is from this perspective and worldview that we consider Afrocentricity as the foundation for understanding black perspectives and contributions to WPA work. We intentionally apply "multidimensional understandings of black thought and practice" with the contributions we feature in this collection. By multidimensional, we mean the inclusion of experiences of black WPAs working at both Historically Black Colleges and Universities (HBCUs) and Predominantly White Institutions (PWIs) to show that while WPAs at both sites are committed to inclusive practices that support students of the African Diaspora, the institutional contexts for taking up that work have very different consequences and implications. Other contributions in this book speak more concretely to pedagogical practices and programmatic policies that are sensitive to the specific interests of black student writers who enroll in our writing courses and programs. For example, such practices include how we assess black students' writing and how we design programmatic outcomes that seek to overcome implicit and explicit biases for black students. Other practices include the types of assignments we design so that black students are permitted to apply their shared collective worldviews to how they see the world and how they communicate within the world. It is an Afrocentric framework, then, that enables us to see existing WPA narratives through a different lens that positions the African worldview as a direct focus, more specifically than previous narratives that view race more broadly.

In laying this foundation, we moreover and explicitly assert that Afrocentric theory does not suggest a separatist discourse that is irrelevant to the lives of those who are not black. In fact, quite the contrary: Countless sources of rhetoric and composition research and scholarship consistently show that Afrocentric theory and pedagogy benefit all students (Richardson; Perryman-Clark, *Afrocentric;* Holmes; Ampadu), and there is certainly no reason that it might not also benefit all of those charged with doing WPA work. More recently, scholars including Arnetha Ball and Ted Lardner and Perryman-Clark have called for specific professional development opportunities concerning Afrocentric teaching and African-centered language pedagogy, and have targeted this call directly at WPAs. Perryman-Clark directly argues that "(1) Afrocentric and language rights pedagogies serve as appropriate occasions for scholarly exploration and teacher training in a writing program and that (2) Afrocentric and language rights pedagogies be included in the general mission and design of writing program curricula" (*Afrocentric* 118–19).

It is from these perspectives, then, that contributors to this collection seek to respond to these calls. Contributors in our collection examine the relationship between issues that focus directly on community members of African descent and the administration of college and university writing programs. This collection centers on conversations surrounding the work of black scholars, teachers, and students because (1) black scholars are significantly underrepresented as writing program administrators (Craig and Perryman-Clark, "Troubling the Boundaries"), (2) the assessment of black students' work in relation to programmatic placement and outcomes is rarely included as a focus of writing assessment work (Inoue and Poe; Inoue; Perryman-Clark, "Who We Are(n')t Assessing"), and (3) limited attention has been paid to the relationship between writing program policies and their direct effects on black students.

Previous work in rhetoric and composition has uncovered the benefits for all students when including Afrocentric, African American–centered, and black-designated pedagogies in our programs (Richardson and Gilyard; Richardson; Perryman-Clark, *Afrocentric*). Additional works call for the need to consider Afrocentric pedagogy in relation to speakers of African American Vernacular English (AAVE)/African American Language (AAL) more directly in writing program administration (Ball and Lardner; Perryman-Clark, *Afrocentric*). Ball and Lardner state:

> A message to those at the writing program administration level . . . calls for the policies and program development that support these activities. We believe writing program administrators will improve educational opportunities of AAVE-speaking students (and all students) by seeking to improve teacher efficacy by initiating and supporting collaborations within and across writing program and institutional boundaries, and by situating efforts aimed at broadening teachers' knowledge of AAVE-related pedagogical issues within collaborative staff-development activities. (177)

Despite this call, limited work has taken up the benefits of Afrocentric pedagogy and African American language in writing program administration. Furthermore, as with Afrocentricity, limited attention has been paid exclusively to blackness at all in WPA scholarship. This collection, then, seeks to shift the focus from race more broadly toward perspectives on blackness in writing program administration.

BOOK ORGANIZATION

The remaining chapters of this book apply Afrocentric approaches to various aspects of WPA work. In Chapter 2, "Administering while Black: Black Women's Labor in the Academy and the 'Position of the Unthought,'" Carmen Kynard recounts experiences with racial microaggressions in relation to antiblack institutional practices. Previously, Perryman-Clark has argued that WPA work by blacks is especially complicated for those who advocate for racial equality, linguistic diversity, and antiracist assessment practices "because doing social justice work on behalf of students poses great risks for the WPA of color's career" ("Who We Are(n't) Assessing" 209). Given the complexities associated with social justice work and the subject positions of those doing this work, we appreciate the insights that Kynard contributes to this collection.

Because positioning black perspectives is a central focus for how we understand writing program administration, we include a direct emphasis on HBCU writing programs. We believe these programs are optimal sites for understanding the contributions of both black WPAs and black students in campus writing programs. In Chapter 3, "A Seat at the Table: Reflections on Writing Studies and HBCU Writing Programs," David F. Green Jr. discusses implications for black WPAs who work at HBCUs. Given the significant role that HBCUs play in shaping how black students succeed, we would be remiss as a field if we did not move their narratives from the margins to the center. In an era when we as public intellectuals are charged with making the case that black lives matter, we must affirm and acknowledge that HBCU pedagogical narratives matter too! In addition to the HBCU experience. In order to emphasize the benefits of Afrocentric work for all students—and, in essence, all WPAs regardless of subject position—we also call on allies to help foster alliances with WPAs of color, especially black WPAs, who administer postsecondary writing programs In Chapter 4, "Forfeiting Privilege for the Cause of Social Justice: Listening to Black WPAs and WPAs of Color Define the Work of White Allyship," Scott Wible extends the conversation to WPA allies who speak to the necessity of moving black WPA perspectives from the margins to the center.

We also offer a theoretical framework for success with black students. In Chapter 5, "Black Student Success Models: Institutional Profiles of Writing Programs," we use the CWPA Framework for Success in Postsecondary Writing as a lens for providing a few principles for the success of African American students in first-year writing programs, something that we argue that CWPA has overlooked. In addition to offering theoretical principles, we use examples of programmatic models from both HBCU and PWI institutions that have employed successful pedagogies with respect to black students. These programmatic models, then, offer tools for WPAs who want to model success at their own program sites.

Speaking of tools, as editors, we conclude this collection by sharing reflections and insights on what WPA looks like when we frame it from an Afrocentric perspective. In Chapter 6, "Reflective Moments: Showcasing University Writing Program Models for Black Student Success," Alexandria Lockett, Shawanda Stewart, Brian Stone, Adrienne Redding, Jonathan Bush, Jeanne LaHaie, Staci, and Collin reflect on the curricular work we have done at both HBCUs and PWIs in support of black student success, building from the framework offered in Chapter 5. By reflecting on the work with student success at our institutional sites, we identify key takeaways for WPA work that pertain to black labor, curriculum development, and power and authority. While reflecting on this work, we also want to provide key tools and pedagogical examples of how our work may benefit black students. As a result, we include electronic profiles from these programmatic profiles at black-perspectives-in-WPA-resources.ncte.org, where we offer curricular materials from these program profiles that affirm black contributions. These curricula include narrative descriptions of writing programs, sample syllabi, sample assignments, and assessment tools aimed to promote student success. Two specific HBCU programs, those at Spelman College and at Huston-Tillotson University, design Afrocentric cultural and linguistic materials to enhance student learning in their writing programs. These materials were also prepared by Alexandria Lockett, of Spelman College, and Shawanda J. Stewart and Brian Stone, of Huston-Tillotson University.

With regard to PWI institutions, we showcase Western Michigan University's ENGL 1050 Intensive (ENGL 1050I) Program. ENGL 1050I is a first-year writing initiative designed to provide students in danger of failing their first-year writing course with a second opportunity to succeed. Two-thirds of the students enrolled in ENGL 1050I are racial minority students, many of whom come from the Detroit Public Schools, a predominantly black school district. In sum, taken together—considering both the work within our print-based collection and the contributions from our electronic resources—we hope that you will come to appreciate these contributions as much as we do, as we aim for the discipline to engage black perspectives on writing program administration with direct emphasis.

In sum, we invite readers to position blackness at the center of the fight against oppressive and racist institutional practices. And we specifically call on allies to assist in this fight. It is our sincerest hope that readers will be equipped with a few tools to resist oppression in university writing programs in the twenty-first century.

WORKS CITED

Als, Hilton. *White Girls*. McSweeny's, 2014.

Ampadu, Lena. "Modeling Orality: African American Rhetorical Practices and the Teaching of Writing." *African American Rhetoric(s): Interdisciplinary Perspectives*, edited by Elaine B. Richardson and Ronald L. Jackson II, Routledge, 2003, pp. 136–54.

Ball, Arnetha F., and Ted Lardner. *African American Literacies Unleashed: Vernacular English and the Composition Classroom*. Southern Illinois UP, 2005.

"Black Women Are the Most Educated Group in the United States." *Shine: For Harriet*, 1 Mar. 2014, shine.forharriet.com/2014/03/black-women-are-most-educated-group-in.html#axzz4CKdMIVaC.

CCAP [Center for College Affordability and Productivity]. "The Disappearing College Male." *Forbes*, 4 May 2015, www.forbes.com/sites/ccap/2015/05/04/the-disappearing-college-male/#2be3e28b50f0.

Cheramie, Deany M. "Sifting through Fifty Years of Change: Writing Program Administration at an Historically Black University." *Historical Studies of Writing Program Administration: Individuals, Communities, and the Formation of a Discipline,* edited by Barbara L'Eplattenier and Lisa Mastrangelo, Parlor Press, 2004, pp. 145–65.

Conference on College Composition and Communication. "CCCC Statement on Ebonics," 31 May 2016, www.ncte.org/cccc/resources/positions/ebonics.

Craig, Collin Lamont, and Staci M. Perryman-Clark. "Troubling the Boundaries: (De) Constructing WPA Identities at the Intersections of Race and Gender." *WPA: Writing Program Administration,* vol. 34, no. 2, Spring 2011, pp. 37–58.

———. "Troubling the Boundaries Revisited: Moving towards Change as Things Stay the Same." *WPA: Writing Program Administration,* vol. 39, no. 2, Spring 2016, pp. 20–26.

Craig, Sherri. "A Story-less Generation: Emergent WPAs of Color and the Loss of Identity through Absent Narratives." *WPA: Writing Program Administration,* vol. 39, no. 2, Spring 2016, pp. 16–20.

Danielle, Britni. "Did You Know Black Women Lead ALL Groups in College Enrollment? Watch This!" *Clutch Magazine,* www.clutchmagonline.com/2014/02/know-black-women-lead-groups-college-enrollment-watch/. Accessed 28 Mar. 2017.

Fulford, Collie. "Hit the Ground Listening: An Ethnographic Approach to New WPA Learning." *WPA: Writing Program Administration,* vol. 35, no. 1, Fall/Winter 2011, pp.159–62.

Graham, Mekada. "Honouring Social Work Principles: Exploring the Connections between Anti-Racist Social Work and African-Centred World Views." *Social Work Education,* vol. 19, no. 5, 2000, pp. 423–36.

Holmes, David G. *Revisiting Racialized Voice: African American Ethos in Language and Literature.* Southern Illinois UP, 2004.

Inoue, Asao B. *Antiracist Writing Assessment Ecologies: Teaching and Assessing Writing for a Socially Just Future.* WAC Clearinghouse and Parlor Press, 2015.

Inoue, Asao B., and Mya Poe. *Racism in Writing Assessment.* Peter Lang, 2012.

Irvine, Jacqueline Jordan. "Afrocentric Education: Critical Questions for Further Considerations." *African-Centered Schooling in Theory and Practice*, edited by Diane S. Pollard and Cheryl S. Ajirotutu, Bergin and Garvey, 2000, pp. 199–210.

Kahn, Seth. "Bad Idea about Writing: Anybody Can Teach It." *Inside Higher Ed*, 7 Aug. 2017, www.insidehighered.com/views/2017/08/07/colleges-should-hire-writing-instructors-right-experience-and-expertise-and-give.

L'Eplattenier, Barbara, and Lisa Mastrangelo, editors. *Historical Studies of Writing Program Administration: Individuals, Communities, and the Formation of a Discipline.* Parlor Press, 2004.

L'Eplattenier, Barbara, Lisa Mastrangelo, and Sherry Rankins-Robertson. Letter from the Editors. *WPA: Writing Program Administration*, vol. 39, no. 2, Spring 2016, pp. 7–8.

National Council of Teachers of English and Conference on College Composition and Communication. "NCTE and CCCC Speak Out against Professor's Treatment by ASU Police." National Council of Teachers of English, 4 July 2014, www.ncte.org/press/issues/anti-racism/asu-letter.

NCTE/CCCC Black Caucus. "NCTE Statement Affirming #BlackLivesMatter." National Council of Teachers of English, Sept. 2015. www.ncte.org/governance/pres-team_9-8-15.

Nearman, Cynthia. "One White Girl's Failed Attempt to Unsilence the Dialogue." *The Promise and Perils of Writing Program Administration*, edited by Theresa Enos and Shane Borrowman, Parlor Press, 2008, pp. 152–64.

Perryman-Clark, Staci M. *Afrocentric Teacher-Research: Rethinking Appropriateness and Inclusion.* Peter Lang, 2013.

———. "Creating a United Front: A Writing Program Administrator's Institutional Investment in Language Rights for Composition Students." *Academic and Professional Writing in an Age of Accountability*, edited by Shirley Wilson Logan and Wayne H. Slater, Southern Illinois UP, 2019, pp. 168–86.

————. "Race, Teaching Assistants, and Student Bullying: Confessions from an African American Pre-tenured WPA." *Defining, Locating, and Addressing Bullying in the WPA Workplace*, edited by Cristyn L. Elder and Bethany Davila, Utah State UP, 2019, forthcoming.

————. "Who We Are(n't) Assessing: Racializing Language and Writing Assessment in Writing Program Administration." *College English*, vol. 79, no. 2, Nov. 2016, pp. 206–11.

"Principles for the Postsecondary Teaching of Writing." *Conference on College Composition and Communication*, Mar. 2015, cccc. ncte.org/cccc/resources/positions/postsecondarywriting.

Richardson, Elaine. *African American Literacies*. Routledge, 2003.

Richardson, Elaine B., and Keith Gilyard. "Students' Right to Possibility: Basic Writing and African American Rhetoric." *Insurrection: Approaches to Resistance in Composition Studies,* edited by Andrea Greenbaum, SUNY P, 2001, pp. 37–51.

Royster, Jacqueline Jones. "When the First Voice You Hear Is Not Your Own." *College Composition and Communication*, vol. 47, no. 1, Feb. 1996, pp. 29–40.

Royster, Jacqueline Jones, and Jean C. Williams. "History in the Spaces Left: African American Presence and Narratives of Composition Studies." *College Composition and Communication*, vol. 50, no. 4, June 1999, pp. 563–84.

Toldson, Ivory A. "Nine Biggest Lies about Black Males and Academic Success." 31 Mar. 2014, *The Root,* theroot.com/9-biggest-lies-about-black-males-and-academic-success-1790875135.

West, Cornel. *Race Matters*. 1993. Beacon Press, 2001.

2

Administering While Black: Black Women's Labor in the Academy and the "Position of the Unthought"

Carmen Kynard

BEFORE I AM A WRITING PROGRAM ADMINISTRATOR (WPA), I am a woman of African descent whose ontology can never be disentangled from a historical memory of racial violence and the black radical tradition. I was never a WPA who just happened to be black. Because the everyday structuring of life in academia functions as a repressive act against blackness, the premise of this chapter and, for that matter, this book, uses the black body as a critical source of sociological imagination of what WPA work has looked like, what it could become, and how we could challenge and resist a neoliberalist higher education within its terms.

In this chapter, I hope to explicitly bind black women's bodies in the academy and WPA to the specific sociohistorical contexts in which those bodies are understood and taken up. With Afro-pessimism as my narrative lens and intellectual foundation, I take up a series of significant memories that have shaped my own racialized experiences of management and organization in higher education. I deliberately compose my memories against a white, linear logic that suggests I can achieve linguistic coherence in a semantic world that expels black thought. In many ways, my memories might arguably be incomplete in recognition of what Afro-pessimism cautions about the necessarily political nature of black creative, intellectual energies: I offer a "metacommentary" rather than the usual tale of the heroism of the lone superman-researcher who arrogantly presumes that his WPA work can offer a prima facie critical intervention in centuries of institutional racism.

AFRO-PESSIMISM AS NARRATIVE LENS
AND INTELLECTUAL FOUNDATION

My narrative politics are heavily influenced by theories of Afro-pessimism perhaps most notable in the works of scholars like Jared Sexton, Saidiya Hartman, Achille Mbembe, Orlando Patterson, Joy James, and Frank Wilderson. This body of scholarship offers me the language for memories and experiences of the academy that are rooted in the distinctiveness of blackness, the perniciousness of racism/white supremacy, and the ongoing failed projects of Western humanities to include blacks in a full humanity. Wilderson's interview with Hartman offers me a most compelling warning when he critiques the ways black scholarship often "peel[s] away from the strength and the terror" (183) of its own evidence in order to offer a final, hope-filled, coherent solution. Without a radical break from the very ideological origins of black subjugation, such easily made solutions will, at best, only cater to the interests of white comfort and white fragility (DiAngelo) and, at worst, operate within the very terms of our oppression. To get right down to it: directing a story to a white readership requires a kind of racial revision in order to make such stories palatable and intelligible inside of a dominant white frame that is not politically transformative for actual black people. Though it will feel very unfamiliar to scholarship related to composition-rhetoric generally and to WPA specifically, Afro-pessimism gives me the theoretical courage to reject the feel-good performative trends of black scholarship in/for a white academy and critically remind myself that I need not—and, in fact, must not—direct my political inquiry to ready-made solutions that will help white teachers and scholars feel better in a world where black death is routinized. Afro-pessimism also moves me beyond white bourgeois and/or market/empirical-driven norms of a university race theory that rarely veers far from acceptable quotations from Michael Omi and Howard Winant's racial formation and into the large body of radical black theorists who have always done race-theory-work. As Sexton argues in "Afro-Pessimism: The Unclear Word," Afro-pessimism is a contemporary radical-intellectual endeavor with theoretical roots deeply planted in the history of black studies. For many of us who research, think, and write about race in the twenty-first century, Afro-pessimism works as our "critical idiom" that connects us back explicitly to black intellectual traditions: from Aimé and Suzanne Césaire's Negritude, to Frantz Fanon's racial slavery, to Sylvia Wynter's critical/cultural humanism, and to critical race theory's grounding in racial realism.

Inspired by Afro-pessimism, I am quite serious about the fact that the kinds of experiences and events that I share in this chapter are deeply grounded in the very routine structure of schooling's antiblackness, where an antipathy to blackness structures our very institutions (Gordon). Violence against black people never needs reason, justification, or provocation. With so much black life excluded from liberty and freedom via slavery, mass incarceration, police brutality, segregated schools, mass poverty, and hypersurveillance, antiblackness is merely gratuitous at the colleges that have historically excluded us and canonized the theories that have rendered us inferior (Wynter, *"Do Not"*). Thus, I attempt to follow through on what Wilderson demands: "a radical racialization of any analysis of positionality" (184), a racialization that refuses to "peel away" from the evidence of what I have lived as WPA/black woman in the academy.

AN EARLY-TENURE MEMORY OF BLACK WOMEN'S BODIES AND POSITIONS IN THE ACADEMY

My official introduction to anti-blackness as the life of the academy began with my first year as a tenure-track professor rather than as a writing program administrator, a title and job that I would have much later. Those early experiences were so deeply lodged in a kind of post-slave geography and plantation logic that they have shaped how I understood the academy from that point forward, my connection to Afro-pessimism, and my later work as a WPA. Antiblackness didn't bypass my studenting days and only show up on the tenure track, but it did take on some decidedly new characteristics.

At my first tenure-track job, during final exams week, all of the departments and programs that "mattered" threw holiday parties (each often having its own theme). You had to be invited to these parties so it should be easy to imagine that this was no small source of anxiety for many junior faculty, who were expected not only to publish intensely but also to be highly visible. If you were a young person of color, you were quite literally confronted with the exclusive membership of an old boy's club at the close of every fall semester. My department had done a lot of recent hiring and so was launching its first holiday party in many years. Decided on by the senior faculty only a week in advance, the party became the responsibility of Debbie, the black woman who worked as our administrative assistant, and who was preemptively and aggressively warned about maintaining an appropriate disposition for such a public holiday venue. When I stopped by her office to see how she was doing after I heard the gossip about her public scolding by white faculty, I immediately saw her watery eyes. Words can never truly convey how that moment affected me. Black women, especially of that generation, do not shed tears publicly in the vicinity of white folk at work. One look at Debbie's face communicated the levels of white toxicity of that department in a way that no other moment had.

I decided that I would try and make Debbie smile, and so the next day I got her some of her favorite candles and made her a CD from a collection of music given to me by my father and amassed from a collection of every winter holiday ballad ever sung by a black person on eight-track tape, cassette tape, video, vinyl, or CD. I compiled a bunch of these songs for Debbie because I knew she would like them. As I was sitting in her office after I gave her this gift, I suggested that she play this CD very loudly. I then devised what I thought was a very clever empirical study. I insisted to Debbie that no single one of the professors in that space actually listened to black people: as she was the help and I was the token— roles that are quite interchangeable—we were only eye candy, so playing these CDs in her office would show that maybe, on a good day, we were vague black noise in the background. Debbie laughed at me until an unknowing "research subject" walked through the door: the main professor who had authorized himself to control the invitation list to the party and dictate how Debbie must organize it. I pretended the CD was mine and popped it into Debbie's CD player, asking him if he wanted to hear it. He said yes and it went straight to a song by Gladys Knight and the Pips (please note that I said: *Gladys Knight. . . and even the Pips, of which there are three*). When I played the song, this professor immediately asked: "Is that Aretha Franklin?" Not missing a beat, I answered with what I thought was the only appropriate response: "Yeah, that's Aretha!" He then said: "Her voice is so distinct you know it anywhere." Now, by this point, Debbie was doing all she could to hide her laughter, and when the professor walked out of the office I reminded her of my original hypothesis and simply said: "See I tole you: Aretha is so damn distinct that she sounds like Gladys Knight. . . and. . . threeeeee Pips! Ain't nobody up in here listening to us!"

Though Debbie and I did not label our discussions of our experiences as Afro-Pessimist theory, everyday theorizing of black bodies *by black bodies* in the academy does not require academic labels. Afro-Pessimism is not the purview of elite black academics where everyday black life gets retrofitted into or inspires traditional academic theorizing. Black women would not survive the academy if they were not theorizing their lives and survival there all of the time (Willoughby-Herard). The Afro-pessimistic rhetoric that fuels my storytelling arc in this chapter is simply a political call to work differently with my memory of this moment. Racism shaped a significant part of my and Debbie's experiences within a set of relations of antiblackness that constituted a racialized psychic life on that campus.

No one seemed to take Debbie's well-being into account in forcing her to organize this party, a source of social capital for the central professors in the department. Debbie was expected to organize this event in about three days, an impossibility at the end of the semester, so I started helping her under one condition: that we would theme the party as a cabaret-rent-party. The price of entry would be an alcoholic beverage, the one thing that I thought absolutely necessary for my own attendance but that the department could not realistically afford. I wouldn't normally admit smuggling alcohol into a party in an essay such as this, but it *is* relevant to the story. On the night of the party, I decked out the conference room with strands of lights and made it really look like a cabaret while Debbie hurried around frantically. When the party started, Debbie stood at the door as the official greeter, and so to relieve her as she refilled coffee cups and food trays I took her place like the little-black-jockey lawn-ornament who greets everyone at the entrance. My Jim Crow/plantation references here are not mere hyperbole since I experience the academy in the way that Katherine McKittrick frames current political conditions of black life—post-slave geographies and plantation logics—and what Hartman further calls the "not-yet-free" twenty-first century ("Position" 192). Not-yet-free made this a different kind of party experience for me, as I will relay in the next section.

AND THE BEAT GOES ON: PLANTATIONS POLITICS/PLANTATION PARTIES

During my black-jockey-greeting duty, I quickly surmised that *everyone* brought a bottle of wine. I started asking folks questions about the wine they were handing to me and, based on their answers, I could figure out whether these white folks had bought a cheap bottle of wine or some of the good stuff. Having learned my own lesson about being a token and not being heard or seen, I knew two things: (1) no one in that room would think that it was strange that only the black women, Debbie and I, were serving and greeting them, and; (2) I was too nearly invisible for anyone to notice if I took *all* of the expensive, good wine bottles and hid them for myself. *I might not have been liberated up in that joint but the wine was certainly gon be.* By the time the party ended, I had *many* bottles, which ended up being easy to transport to my office because, of course, it was just Debbie and I staying late and cleaning up the place (the work of the help/token is never done).

In this description of my mammified introduction to tenured work in the academy, I am quite purposefully relying on the image (and history) of black women as domestic servants/mammies as one of the most prevalent ways in which black women's bodies have been historically and publicly consumed and sexualized since slavery. These images have sustained the exploitation and denigration of black women's bodies, fully denying us a right to a personhood and a humanity of our own. Given the context of post-slave societies, plantation logics (McKittrick), and the not-yet-free twenty-first century (Hartman), the mammy is more than just a stereotype, media representation, or dominant image, but a fundamental material organization of race, labor, and power (Wallace-Sanders). As a result, I am suggesting, the racial authority of black women's work as university faculty and staff is hypermediated by this historical role of the mammy (Wilson). The mammy role is further inscribed in our work as university administrators, given the almost perfunctory assumption (however inaccurate) that administrative work in higher education is service, a social expectation that further chains black women's bodies in specific ways. Before I had finished my first semester on the tenure track, I could add a long list of other college tasks to my dossier that no white faculty member in my department could: party organizer, food preparer, hostess, greeter, server, and cleanup crew. While my white colleagues did not recognize this labor, other black women on campus surely did.

I came in the morning after the party to finish cleanup and as I was about to leave for the day, Debbie asked me to read my emails first. When I went to my inbox, I saw an email from every black woman who was an administrative assistant on the campus who had apparently heard of my antics from Debbie (including a wide array of things omitted from this essay) and so invited me to their program's party. This, in sum, meant that I had an invitation to every single holiday party on that campus from the provost's office to the financial aid department because, after all, it was black women running all this stuff. I don't think I can adequately describe the look on my colleagues' faces when they saw me appear at each party and then leave for parties to which they were not invited. And no one seemed to really wonder how or why I greeted every single black woman who had invited me with a very special party favor:

an ornamental bag, obviously containing a bottle of wine, and in this case, some of the most expensive wine available on that campus, which the white faculty themselves had of course purchased.

I am spending a considerable amount of time on this memory because I want to highlight the everydayness of the exploitive, racialized service and domesticity that are expected of black women in the academy, all intimately connected to the ways in which blackness and sexuality have structured the very core of western modernity (Weheliye; Hammonds). This mammification of our bodies and labor was never hidden, masked, or subtle. Racism was obvious all day, every day, part of how the institution imagined itself and part of how the daily routines of campus life were performed (Gilmore, "Public"). What I am also suggesting is that the institutional context that I have perhaps painstakingly described is the context in which the administrative bodies and work of black women gets understood also.

There is another critical aspect of this opening memory: each and every single professor in that department at my first tenure-track job did research related to impoverished black youth since that campus's research mission was explicitly connected to the working-class/working-poor black community that housed us. These folk who could so readily see Debbie and me as their diminutive servants were also writing about *us* and, in fact, there was no real contradiction between maintaining racial hierarchies and being published under the guise of scholarship that dismantles such hierarchies. Treating blackness as just another marginalized identity, the professors of that department advanced the cause of reform and integration without rigorous attention to the specificity of anti-blackness and what Loïc Wacquant would call the advanced marginality of the black masses all around us. If we take Afro-pessimism seriously, then we can see that there really is no contradiction in "researching" about/for justice in black communities from the confines of institutions that render their bodies subject to invisible servitude. The ongoing material relations of slavery mean ultimately that, as Hartman argues, you can "choose to do what you wish with the Black body," for good or bad (188). I am reminded of how many WPA scholars consider themselves activist and cast their policies and programs within the terms of social justice while the specific ways institutional racism shapes their campuses rarely makes a blip in that research, research that they nonetheless insist represents transformative programming. My first tenure-track job taught me well: I could be expected to diminutively serve white people while they published scholarship claiming to save me.

That first semester showed me everything I needed to know about black women faculty, because nothing ever really improved (Kynard). In more ways than I could ever have imagined, my first semester prepared me for my next professional experience, as a writing program administrator at a large nonelite private university in a large Northeastern Metropolitan center. As a woman of color directing a program, who thinks of herself within the terms of radical black feminist subjectivity, I do not have the luxury of ignoring the social and material practices of institutional racism that reproduces itself by denigrating bodies of color in higher education. WPA work has looked no different from the other racist realities I have navigated.

BLACK WOMEN AS WPA MAMMIES,
ON AND OFF CAMPUS: PART I

While I have valued the research/activism showing us that today's corporatized universities unleash unchecked levels of class exploitation, that body of work has not offered adequate insights into black women's lives and WPA experiences. As Staci Perryman-Clark and Collin Craig argue in their introduction to this collection as well as in their larger body of work (see, for example, "Troubling the Boundaries" and "Troubling the Boundaries Revisited"), we have not yet fully examined racialized narratives of blackness in the context of WPA work and leadership in our field. There are specific material relations, structural organizing tools, and practices of knowledge production in white-masculine, hypermanaged universities that take unique forms in the presence of black women's bodies as administrators in these spaces. As a black woman and previous director of a writing program at that large urban, nonelite, private university (which boasted the third-most-diverse student population in the nation), I examine the mammy stereotype of black women as more than just a metaphor for my storytelling arc here, but as an actual social mechanism that attempts to reproduce a certain kind of labor for black women (Wallace-Sanders). While my experiences as a WPA do not differ drastically from my experiences as a black woman/professor in the academy, the apparatus of administration in hypermanaged universities brings the academy's antiblackness into stunning view when black women's work is at the center of the narrative.

My early days as a WPA were, to put it mildly, quite difficult. On my very first day on campus, one white male faculty member in the program forthrightly insisted on meeting with me one-on-one after I had participated in almost eight hours of orientation activities. His purpose, as he saw it, was to dictate all of the things that I needed to do. Thus, my first task on the same day that I was officially "on payroll" as a WPA was to dissipate a white man's anger directly targeted at me. This interaction could hardly be characterized as anything other than me mammying him up until the point where he felt comforted that I would hear his concerns. I managed his outbursts simply because far too many of the other white faculty saw him as their mouthpiece and ringleader.

One of my first lessons as a WPA was that white men could freely antagonize black women but when they make a single misstep with a white man, all bets are off. When this same white male faculty member stepped out of line with a white male WPA, he was stripped of his leadership roles and alienated to the point that he left the program. None of these events were surprising to me, as I know to expect open hostility from white men as soon as I arrive on a new college campus, before I even unpack my boxes, despite the fact that I am a person who generally keeps to herself unless I really know you. I have had to learn to manage white male aggressiveness in the academy in ways that are really no different from knowing what to do when the NYPD profiles me, pulls me over, and digs through my bags at the subway station. As a black woman WPA, you constantly manage aggression toward your position as administrator *alongside* your position as a woman professor of color.

It was no surprise either that many of the first-year writing (FYW) faculty would say all kindsa crazy mess to me when I first arrived, despite the fact that I received more of their votes than other candidates after my interview process. In hindsight, I should have asked every administrator I met during my campus visit for their strategies for dealing with white fall-out when a black woman WPA does not merely get the job but actually shows up for it. In that way, I could have gotten a better sense of the racial politics of the space. I wonder if that would have helped or replaced the usual response when I voiced concerns: reminders that I was hired and expected to serve as a domineering matriarch (which was once even related to a story that I had told about my black grandmother in the rural Jim Crow South).

I knew that getting faculty to talk with me and trust me as a WPA was an arduous task but if you are a black woman that task takes longer with more roadblocks set against you. While some things never changed, however, what was transformable were faculty expectations that I teach them the histories and culturally relevant pedagogies related to students of color. Instead, we treated this as inquiry research in writing/thinking groups among ourselves. In the end, that small group were the faculty currently teaching in the program whom I ended up working alongside most closely.

I question whether the slow gains (if any) of my work as a WPA and the psychological assaults of working with those committed to the demise of the black body was worth the drain on my time and energy. It's an ontological experience unaccounted for in de-racialized notions of political change and activism in WPA work. The antagonism didn't just come from within the writing program, though. Off-campus and extradepartmental folk acted the fool too.

BLACK WOMEN AS WPA MAMMIES, ON AND OFF CAMPUS: PART II

When I need to explain to my undergraduate students how race, black feminism, and rhetoric intersect, I tell them about my experiences as a WPA and they get it right away. I explain to them that it is quite typical as a WPA to receive constant emails from other college administrators and staff across the nation as well as many requests from other offices on campus, all of whom might need help with a variety of staffing or resource issues. With the exception of those folk (usually of color) who were my close friends, there was *no* single instance where a white person ever emailed me directly, and this included *many* other WPAs across the country. On each occasion, white people would either: (1) email a white male above me *or* side-by-side with me in rank rather than reach out to me at all; or (2) email me but cc a whole posse of white folk and not speak directly with me in the email. This means that I never once interacted with any national or local white actor needing the help of my program who had the ability to see me as a person of authority (see Wallace et al.). They all needed to authorize a white man either before or while they talked with me. The multiple websites with me listed as the director, photo included, or the big sign on my door labeling me as director seemingly made no difference. This might not be so extreme except for one striking fact: each of these emails that were not directed to me requested labor, time, and attention that only I could provide.

I tell this story to my students to ask them to decide who they will be when they craft words and rhetoric in a world that normalizes the exploitation of their bodies and yet refuses to see and hear them. This has sometimes stirred tremendous emotion in my classes. In a recent experience, an older student, an AfroLatina woman who does domestic work at a local hospital, started crying when I told this story and many other women of color followed. As part of the custodial staff at the hospital, this student described the dehumanizing treatment toward her from white patients and staff and was really distraught about her erroneous assumption that a college degree (given that I had obtained the highest level with a PhD) would curb the white disrespect that was constantly targeting her. I assure my students that a degree will not curb disrespect; you have to do that yourself. Just because white folk give you orders don't mean you have to listen and follow. You simply fight back in whatever ways you can at any given moment.

When white folk emailed white men when they were seeking my help, these men often cc'd me in their responses and then went ahead and answered the emailer's queries themselves, most times with misinformation. There is a special expression for this latter foolishness: *all up in the Kool-Aid but don't know the flava.* I share this to counter any false impression that all this white male racial authority actually meant accuracy or competence. Unless it was really detrimental to faculty, I never corrected the misinformation and let the emailers make fools of themselves with their inaccuracies. I also did not respond to emailers who asked for (or sometimes demanded) my work, talking about me but never to me, as if I were invisible. The folk who directly came at me foul-mouthed after my lack of response simply got their feelings hurt for their racialized behaviors in some of the most eloquent emails that I have ever written in my career. It took some folk longer than others, but all these white folk—on campus, at other campuses, and in the field—learned real fast that if they needed me for something, they couldn't simply tell a white man to order my (invisibilized) labor and pretend not to see me.

These labor experiences *profoundly* shaped how I understood myself as a WPA; how I understood the time and place in which I worked; how I saw white people's perception of my person and body; how I navigated my world and work; and whom I trusted. Put most simply, given this example: I speak and act from a place where I grant myowndamnself authority in lily-white spaces where no one else does given the ongoing psychosocial/racial need to reproduce my work and body as mammy. If you ain't gon bother to see me, you best make sure you don't ever need me. These moments of nonrecognition in my WPA experience compelled me to ask, "What might it mean to be a member of a professional community that does not recognize black folk as having authority or co-participation, only as nameless and invisible labor?" And if white folk can't recognize me as equal or even see me as *there,* then the students who look like me don't have a chance in hell in the programs that we run, no matter how many diversity position statements we write or how much we insist we are activist WPAs.

Because so many WPAs have gone into upper-level administration in deans' and provosts' offices, it might seem that there is greater institutional support for writing programs and WPAs at such colleges. This is not always the case, as former WPAs-turned-deans-and-provosts (for the sake of this essay, I will call them Super-WPAs) can be found across the country implementing and enculturating racist curriculum and policy. The Super-WPAs can also sometimes add further stress to the whitenized project of WPA work for black women. Faculty in the writing program will often get coerced into locating the newly risen (often white and/or male) bodies of the Super-WPAs as a new site of authority where, quite literally, financial rewards and professional gain are meted out to them.

Though I was the director of FYW, for instance, the Super-WPA frequently informed the tenure-track faculty of the program to bypass reading the research of composition-rhetoric, publishing in the field, or attending the field's conferences. Instead, many of the faculty were encouraged to focus on their own alternative research and fields that had no intersection with composition-rhetoric studies. While it is no surprise that other faculty in the liberal arts might hold this disdain for composition studies, these words of advice came from the Super-WPA who overdirected my program in such a way that tenure in FYW did not require any real interest in or knowledge *about* first-year writing, a culture that I was attempting to shape. I had to spend an inordinate amount of time observing classrooms for official tenure and promotion paperwork, work with faculty on pedagogy, fight other administrators and faculty when FYW faculty were treated unfairly (many of whom would never have done the same for someone like me), sit on endless tenure review committees, and direct searches—all of this work for a program whose ideological underpinnings had little to do with composition theory because the Super-WPA saw it so. To be sure, these programmatic issues signal a general, programmatic hot mess, but when you add race and a black woman WPA to the mix, you move that hot mess from the pan into the fire.

At one point, FYW faculty—and no other faculty on the campus—were each offered $2,500 of discretionary funds from the Super-WPA as long as they could produce receipts for books, membership in professional societies, and the like for him. I had no idea these funds had even been distributed until I heard faculty in the hallways talking about the ways they would refund items purchased at Amazon and pocket the cash. One faculty member, someone I consider an ally and good friend, was so offended by the entire situation that she offered me part of her funds as well as offering a part to a faculty member who had left the program a few weeks before. Besides this general breach of ethics in doling out tens of thousands of dollars this way, such moves by the Super-WPA coerced faculty into silence and situated white male power as the only locus of importance. Even when I attempted to tell other campus figures what was happening (since obviously their junior faculty were not given such funds), the response was only laughter at what the Super-WPA was able to get away with, almost as if in bro-mantic awe of the power of their white comrade.

These vestiges of white power were, of course, not possible without the Super-WPA's deployment of young white women, self-proclaimed feminism notwithstanding, to provide information about all events and any persons under my leadership who were regarded as unruly or ungrateful. On numerous occasions, I had to inform pretenured faculty, adjuncts, and graduate students, particularly those of color, that all of their words were being transmitted directly back to the Super-WPA and, therefore, the provost's/dean's office. It was their choice ultimately on the public rhetorics they chose to craft in these meetings, but everyone needed to know the specific publics who were involved for the sake of greater transparency. As part of my own strategy, I made sure to say the things that I wanted to get back to the Super-WPA, sometimes even satirically exaggerated for full effect. *Give em sumthin to talk about* was my overarching goal, come what may. In turn, these cooperative white women, whose bid for tenure was, at best, shaky, secured their own privilege and standing within the program.

Herein lies the lesson about plantation logics. In the tradition of Afro-pessimism, I treat slavery and the mammy figure as a relational dynamic and not as a specific event, moment in time, or place (Wilderson, Patterson). This compels me to remind myself and other WPA/researchers like me: just because you routinely clean, stock, organize, and run the place does not mean that white folk will ever perceive you as belonging there and having a real part of it (Ahmed). While the shock-and-awe campaigns of the Super-WPA might seem a bit over the top, they were the norm in my experience as a WPA. Whether it was the shock-and-awe campaign of the Super-WPA or the invisibility to fellow WPAs across the county and other administrators on campus, a full-blown constellation of racialized events act simultaneously to deliberately discredit and mock a black woman's leadership while superexploiting every ounce of her labor. These are not the mean, individual acts of a few morally misguided souls. Higher education strategically contains a diverse pool of faculty such that whiteness stays on top. WPA gets as ingrained with institutional racism as any other space and relies on the mammification of black women just as does any other racialized project.

MAMMIES AND THE CIRCULATION OF BLACK WOMEN'S BODIES . . . "BEFO' DA WAH" AND DURING WPA

Understanding the history of the mammy is critical here in my representations of black women as professors, scholars, and university administrators. In post-emancipation history, in 1889 to be specific, Chris Rutt and Charles Underwood invented the image of Aunt Jemima for their first ready-made pancake mix. This image of a servile African American woman soon became one of the most popular and enduring forms of American marketing. Aunt Jemima was originally written as a jolly ex-slave who lived on a Louisiana plantation and made legendary flapjacks in the days "befo' de wah"—a black woman who lived to do nothing but nurture, clean, and cook for whites. There was even an "Aunt Jemima's Pancake House" with a black woman dressed in full costume for years at Disneyland. "Pancake Days is Happy Days" is one of the slogans used in a popular print ad dating back to 1938 with the caption: "Only wif my magic recipe can you turn out dese tender, 'licious, jiffy-quick pancakes dat makes yo' family happy" (McElya).

Aunt Jemima, as the quintessential mammy, is about more than just "tender, 'licious, jiffy-quick pancakes" and racist imagery, though; these flapjacks buttressed racial hierarchy. At the turn of the twentieth century, the new white middle class had fewer servants and more modernized kitchens and learned to cope with their new situation with what became commonly known as a "slave in a box." Purchasing an Aunt Jemima pancake mix was like buying the labor of a black servant and, thereby, maintaining white superiority. This new Aunt-Jemima-in-a-Box offered white families the nostalgia of the Old South, with its presumed happy slaves and benevolent white masters alongside continued access to black women's labor. White families, especially white housewives, could buy this product and thereby the fantasy of being a mistress/master again to a house full of black slave labor (Manring). Borrowing from the terminology of Patricia Hill Collins, black feminist thinkers have continually examined this "controlling image" of the mammy for the ways that it captures dominant representations of the ideal black female relationship to white power (Wallace-Sanders). Even images of Mammy as an authority figure and, sometimes, sole humanitarian/moral character in white homes (as in William Faulkner's novels) highlight Mammy's knowing her place as an obedient servant.

I do not mean to suggest here that the work of black women in slavery bears a direct relationship to black women's status and WPA work today. However, I reject any notion that the "mammy" is merely an image or stereotype or that black emancipation from slavery signaled a real break from this content of slavery (Spillers; James). I do not treat white supremacy as a single, coherent, unified occurrence but as a set of histories and institutions that continually (re)arrange black subjugation (Martinot and Sexton). So, yes, slavery is over, but slave relations are not; newer forms of racial domination merely replace older forms with black women's abject servitude as a mutating constant in what Alexander Weheliye calls racializing assemblages that "typify different manifestations of enfleshment" (118). As Tiffany Willoughby-Herard argues, framing the experiences of women faculty of color through the controlling image of the mammy illuminates a specific set of realities for black women in the academy: "We are expected to labor for historical white institutions and, in the process, not only show subservience and deference but also express extraordinary appreciation (and implicit approval) for the institution we serve" (159). Black women's WPA work thus represents specific assemblages of race and domination in the academy.

And, of course, I am not suggesting that people literally wanted me to roll out Aunt Jemima's pancake batter as their WPA (although, at times, I did wonder). Instead, I like to think in the terms that Wynter uses in her remix of Helen Fein's work. In her essay, "'No Humans Involved': An Open Letter to My Colleagues," written right after the acquittal of the police officers who brutally beat Rodney King in 1992, Wynter argues that you need to look to the decades and centuries preceding a group's denigration to see and understand how the dominant group has perpetuated a regime that marks a subordinated group as outside of the "sanctified universe of obligation." Hers is a theoretical position that protects black women like me (who see this mammy image as recurring) from the claims that we are simplifying history by saying racism today is the same as racism years before. No, we can't say that today's mammy images are the "exact same" as the 1938 "Pancake Days is Happy Days" ads, but we *can* say that the "universe of sanctified obligation" renders my body as WPA as wholly exploitable but not as capable of equal participation in the making of knowledge on campus or in the wider field. WPA operationalized the same dynamics as when I stood at the door of a holiday party at my first tenure-track job, greeting the white professors on campus as a servant, with seemingly very few able to recognize me as a colleague or question the racial dynamics of the campus.

BLACK WOMEN WPA AND THE "POSITION OF THE UNTHOUGHT"

The daily experiences that are unique to black women faculty's bodies on college campuses offer critical insights. At a time when structures and processes of today's corporate universities oppress us all, we need multiple perspectives to do the work at hand. Black women will be critical, not as desexualized maids in the kitchen in order to maintain the illusion of white superiority, but as people who know what it means to fight back every day, each day in systems that have never offered fairness or equity. That's just not an experience or theoretical grounding that everyone has had.

Obviously, I could have taken this essay in many different directions. I could have delineated all of the processes and projects I implemented as a WPA as a kind of blueprint for navigating higher education's version of the "white supremacist avant-garde" (Martinot and Sexton). Or, I could have done a drive-by literature review of a mass of extant WPA literature and its inability to offer relevance or insight about black women's bodies who engage in that work. Both options mean I would basically do what we always do: give white folk the most time and space in the field. I opted against these modes of discourse and organization. Instead, I wanted to take the work of a black woman's narrative of WPA very seriously and root that work in *black theory*, thereby necessitating real interdisciplinarity/transdisciplinarity. I want to stay focused on the kind of criticality that Hartman presents when she asks about crafting/enabling a narrative that speaks to black women's positions when they have never even been fully named—a social condition that she so brilliantly describes as occupying "the position of the unthought" ("Position" 185).

Running implicitly through this chapter is a desire for something more than mere inclusion within the racially limited set of possibilities that WPA research theoretically provides. To borrow from Martinot and Sexton, our "language of alternatives" often gets overrun by a political discourse that assumes our current system needs reform rather than radical departures from our current projects (170). Afro-pessimism pushes me to understand racial violence as a rule, so we cannot assume the possibility of reform. To do so means that we think the system is working and just needs some tweaking. Most important, Afro-pessimism evokes a renewed energy for me to contextualize antiblackness as a "historically varying" phenomenon rooted in what Wynter would see as our current episteme "while maintaining the claim that slavery is here and now"

(Sexton, "Afro-Pessimism"). Treated as what Sexton calls a "poetics and politics" and "political ontology," Afro-pessimism bears witness to the ways that blackness interrupts and disrupts every claim and theory of identity formation, marginalization, and difference that we formulate.

I see the academy from the terms of Sexton's critique of "liberalism's social democracy" ("Racial Profiling") in that it merely pretends it is interested in justice and remedies for injustice. Reconstructing white institutions (or simply accepting more students of color or hiring more faculty and WPAs of color) is not the same as dismantling racial violence. The task then is to argue for the pervasive ordinariness of white supremacy and offer analyses that unwaveringly remind us about that banality, no matter how uncomfortable or apprehensive it will make us. If racial violence is structural and not accidental or incidental, then white supremacy is just a mundane affair in which the actors who benefit most acquiesce to race, whiteness, and power almost reflexively. White supremacy has no logic, only an excessive repetition that gives it a networking of practices. Black women's bodies in a history rooted in slavery thus offer us distinct insights into race, the academy, and WPA work.

By way of a closing, I want to come back to the counterexpressive energies of black subordinated groups in academic institutions. Though I left WPA work at my institution and remain on the fence about whether I can trust another institution to avoid the superexploitation of my black woman's labor/body as a WPA ever again, there were certainly maroon/fugitive communities (Harney and Moten) in that space where colleagues whom I miss dearly did deep dialogue and work on race, power, and teaching. These interactions were hidden far away from the white surveillance gaze and surpass much of the other such work I have encountered in the academy.

Though the categories imposed onto black women's labor/black women WPAs as oppressed servants remains constant, we would miss the fuller picture if we didn't see all the seized opportunities and pleasures to be found in rebelling against these categories, which even included, in my case, sometimes looting the good wine. Black consciousness always contests white institutions and, thereby, recreates lifestyles/mindstyles in hideaway and remote spaces (Harney and Moten). In the worst-case scenario, dominant whiteness and WPA research/practice may fully merge to become just another category against which black women must rebel. But even if that does happen, we will still create counterplantation spaces where black fugitive radicals can go to be free.

WORKS CITED

Ahmed, Sara. "Embodying Diversity: Problems and Paradoxes for Black Feminists." *Race, Ethnicity, and Education*, vol. 12, no. 1, 2009, pp. 41–52.

Collins, Patricia Hill. *Black Feminist Thought: Knowledge, Consciousness, and the Politics of Empowerment*. Routledge, 1991.

Craig, Collin Lamont, and Staci M. Perryman-Clark . "Troubling the Boundaries: (De) Constructing WPA Identities at the Intersections of Race and Gender." *WPA: Writing Program Administration*, vol. 34, no. 2, Spring 2011, pp. 37–58.

———. "Troubling the Boundaries Revisited: Moving towards Change as Things Stay the Same." *WPA: Writing Program Administration*, vol. 39, no. 2, Spring 2016, pp. 20–26.

DiAngelo, Robin J. "I'm Leaving!": White Fragility in Racial Dialogues." *Inclusion in Urban Educational Environments: Addressing Issues of Diversity, Equity, and Social Justice*, edited by Denise E. Armstrong and Brenda J. McMahon. Information Age Publishing, 2006, pp. 213–40.

———. "White Fragility." *International Journal of Critical Pedagogy*, vol. 3, no. 3, 2011, pp. 54–70.

Gilmore, Ruth Wilson. "Fatal Couplings of Power and Difference: Notes on Racism and Geography." *The Professional Geographer*, vol. 54, no. 1, 2002, pp. 15–24.

———. "Public Enemies and Private Intellectuals: Apartheid USA." *Race and Class*, vol. 35, no. 1, July 1993, pp. 69–78.

Gordon, Lewis R. *Bad Faith and Antiblack Racism*. Humanities Press, 1995.

Gutiérrez y Muhs, Gabriella, Yolanda Flores Niemann, Carmen G. González, and Angela P. Harris, editors. *Presumed Incompetent: The Intersections of Race and Class for Women in Academia*. Utah State UP, 2012

Hammonds, Evelynn M. "Toward a Genealogy of Black Female Sexuality: The Problematic of Silence." *Feminist Genealogies, Colonial Legacies, Democratic Futures,* edited by M. Jacqui Alexander and Chandra Talpade Mohanty, Routledge, 1997, pp. 170–82.

Harney, Stefano, and Fred Moten. *The Undercommons: Fugitive Planning and Black Study.* Autonomedia, 2013.

Hartman, Saidiya V. "'The Position of the Unthought: An Interview by Frank B. Wilderson, III." *Qui Parle,* vol. 13, no. 2, Spring–Summer 2003, pp. 183–201.

———. *Scenes of Subjection: Terror, Slavery, and Self-Making in Nineteenth-Century America.* Oxford University Press, 1997.

James, Joy. *Imprisoned Intellectuals: America's Political Prisoners Write on Life, Liberation, and Rebellion.* Rowman & Littlefield, 2003.

Kynard, Carmen. "From Candy Girls to Cyber Sista-Cipher: Narrating Black Females' Color-Consciousness and Counterstories in and out of School." *Harvard Educational Review.* vol. 80, no. 1, Spring 2010, pp. 30–52.

Manring, M. M. *Slave in a Box: The Strange Career of Aunt Jemima.* UP of Virginia, 1998.

Martinot, Steve, and Jared Sexton. "The Avant-Garde of White Supremacy." *Social Identities,* vol. 9, no. 2, 2003, pp. 169–81.

Mbembe, Achille. *On the Postcolony.* U of California P, 2001.

McElya, Micki. *Clinging to Mammy: The Faithful Slave in Twentieth-Century America.* Harvard UP, 2007.

McKittrick, Katherine. *Demonic Grounds: Black Women and the Cartographies of Struggle.* U of Minnesota P, 2006.

———. "On Plantations, Prisons, and a Black Sense of Place." *Social and Cultural Geography,* vol. 12, no. 8, 2011, pp. 947–63.

Omi, Michael, and Howard Winant. *Racial Formation in the United States.* 3rd ed., Routledge, 2015.

Patterson, Orlando. *Slavery and Social Death: A Comparative Study.* Harvard UP, 1982.

Sexton, Jared. "Afro-Pessimism: The Unclear Word." *Rhizomes: Cultural Studies in Emerging Knowledge,* vol. 29, 2016, www.rhizomes.net/issue29/sexton.html.

———. *Amalgamation Schemes: Antiblackness and the Critique of Multiracialism.* U of Minnesota P, 2008.

———. "Racial Profiling and the Societies of Control." *Warfare in the American Homeland: Policing and Prison in a Penal Democracy,* edited by Joy James, Duke UP, 2007, pp. 197–218.

Spillers, Hortense J. *Black, White, and in Color: Essays on American Literature and Culture.* U of Chicago P, 2003.

Wacquant, Loïc. "From Slavery to Mass Incarceration: Rethinking the 'Race Question' in the U.S." *New Left Review,* no. 13, Jan.–Feb. 2002, pp. 41–60.

Wallace, Sherri L., Sharon E. Moore, Linda L. Wilson, and Brenda G. Hart. "African American Women in the Academy: Quelling the Myth of Presumed Incompetence." Gutiérrez y Muhs, Niemann, González, and Harris, pp. 421–38.

Wallace-Sanders, Kimberly. *Mammy: A Century of Race, Gender, and Southern Memory.* U of Michigan P, 2008.

Weheliye, Alexander G. *Habeas Viscus: Racializing Assemblages, Biopolitics, and Black Feminist Theories of the Human.* Duke UP, 2014.

Wilderson, Frank, III. *Red, White and Black: Cinema and the Structure of U.S. Antagonisms.* Duke UP, 2010.

Willoughby-Herard, Tiffany. "Mammy No More/Mammy Forever: The Stakes and Costs of Teaching Our Colleagues." *The Truly Diverse Faculty: New Dialogues in American Higher Education,* edited by Stephanie A. Fryberg and Ernesto Javier Martínez, Palgrave, 2014, pp. 157–91.

Wilson, Sherrée. "They Forgot Mammy Had a Brain." Gutiérrez y Muhs, Niemann, González, and Harris, pp. 65–77.

Wynter, Sylvia. *"Do Not Call Us Negros": How Multicultural Textbooks Perpetuate Racism.* Aspire Books, 1990.

———. "'No Humans Involved': An Open Letter to My Colleagues." *Forum N.H.I.: Knowledge for the Twenty-First Century,* vol. 1, no. 1, 1994, pp. 42–72.

3

A Seat at the Table: Reflections on Writing Studies and HBCU Writing Programs

David F. Green Jr.

I SAY THIS NOT TO BE BOLD OR SHOCKING, BUT race remains central to my experience as a junior Writing Program Administrator (WPA) and remains connected to a number of interactions and ideas about writing that shape my writing program. Yes, race is a social construct, one with an interesting legacy that is always moving in concert with nationalistic beliefs about power and individual rights; it is also linked to the ways we talk about cultural and rhetorical traditions. More specifically, it is linked to how certain traditions and forms of knowledge are valued. Within WPA scholarship there remains a dearth in critical perspectives that recognize and advocate for ways of integrating cultural perspectives into the work of writing programs at the level of teacher training, curricular outcomes, and policy decisions. The goal for this essay is to add to the body of WPA scholarship by considering how black rhetorical practices aid formal composition instruction and theories of WPA work.

Specifically, I am interested in the ways that African American rhetorical traditions can be deployed to rethink certain approaches to the teaching of writing. My aim is to show how we might better integrate hip-hop rhetorical forms that derive from black culture into how writing programs are shaped. Of particular value in this effort is the concept of the cypher. The cypher is a spatial and conceptual metaphor drawn from hip-hop culture that defines an imagined and physical space used to prepare others to think through complex networks of competing thoughts. Cyphers, at their best, provide pathways for contemplating how publics read and remember together, as well as how such interpretive work helps to address difference as a social, cultural, and material reality of all writing instruction.

Such an interest in the cypher metaphor originates from a desire to better understand my own experiences as an African American professor of rhetoric and writing, and to help myself gauge how I choose to lead my department's writing program. In "Disciplinary Narratives 1980–2000: A Cultural Rhetoric Approach," Jim Zebroski asks the intriguing question, "How does analyzing cultural rhetoric help us to imagine other ways of writing our disciplinary stories?" (22). What I hear in the question is a desire to understand writing and textual production as a variegated and multicultural practice, one that is always informed by the numerous literacies brought to any given writing occasion. In other words, in what other ways might we understand the movements, values, and identities shaping the history of rhetoric and composition? I highlight Zebroski's question because I believe it is central to opening up our attention to cultural rhetoric's value to WPA work. The cypher, in particular, draws attention to an alternate rhetorical tradition, a tradition that has informed and continues to inform how our students compose and how program stakeholders value what students bring to and compose in our writing programs.

As a WPA, any work toward addressing race specifically, and difference more broadly, requires approaches and strategies that work to simultaneously raise the consciousness of writing instructors and identify macrolevel practices that reinforce racist logics embedded in the teaching and assessment of students. As Carmen Kynard notes in "Teaching while Black: Witnessing and Countering Disciplinary Whiteness, Racial Violence, and University Race-Management," racist logics are a part of the very "progress narratives" scholars often tell about the field of rhetoric and composition, whether intentionally or unintentionally (3). For her, we are a part of the problem unless we begin to interrogate the ways that university culture and writing courses maintain racism or racist logics that frame and reinforce campus political life.

It is this context, this concern, that I concentrate on the most recent movement in our field, "writing about writing," and suggest approaches so its goals honor and acknowledge race as a central construct shaping the types of conversations about writing that benefit a broad spectrum of writers. I argue that an embrace of cultural writing traditions might expand the ways "writing about writing" (WAW) approaches are conceived of and presented to students. Because the WAW movement evolves out of writing studies, and because it has gained traction within the field as a way of thinking about how we train students to think about writing, writing programs that value cultural rhetoric and antiracist teaching can use the framing of an expanded WAW to explore different concepts or traditions. I then shift to a focus on the *Visions and Cyphers* textbook used in first-year writing at the historically black university where I work as the WPA. The book highlights a way of situating conversations "about writing" in the field using the cypher as a guiding approach. I then close out with a discussion of how cyphers aid in addressing the "racial realism" Kynard highlights as necessary to addressing the racist practices embedded in the ways that writing instruction and university culture often operate.

One final note before beginning: The title for this essay is in part borrowed from the critically acclaimed album by singer Solange Knowles, *A Seat at the Table,* because the album represents an imaginative response to institutional and social constraints experienced by a black woman navigating race within a number of social spheres. On the album Knowles shares numerous perspectives on the way race has shaped the careers and attitudes of a number of people. In fact, through her music and interludes on the album, she constructs a veritable cypher among her parents, rapper Master P, and herself as they discuss their experiences expressing a black subjectivity often challenged by a largely white music industry and other social institutions that have undermined their expressive identities. The album itself weaves and constructs fluid celebrations of critical black subjectivities.

Such an approach reminds me of Jacqueline Royster's "When the First Voice You Hear Is Not Your Own," which, among other topics, frames the importance of culture and subjectivity for under-

standing how and when one chooses to articulate his or her dispositions, as well as the rich traditions and values from which one draws
to articulate them. In the essay, Royster explains,

> Those of us who love our communities, we think, most deep-
> ly, most uncompromisingly, without reservation for what
> they are and also are not, must set aside our misgivings about
> strangers in the interest of the possibility of deeper under-
> standing (and for the more idealistic among us, the possibility
> of global peace). Those of us who hold these communities to
> our hearts, protect them, and embrace them; those who want
> to preserve the goodness of the minds and souls in them;
> those who want to preserve consciously, critically, and also
> lovingly the record of good work within them must take high
> risk and give over the exclusivity of our rights to know. (33)

What I gather from Royster and Knowles is a way of thinking about
black cultural dispositions toward writing and what they might
mean for the current discussions of the WAW movement within
the field. This, for me, has important consequences for how institutions and writing programs are designed to serve specific minority
populations (populations that bring with them important histories
of writing), and how they decide to define and discuss writing with
students.

RETHINKING WAW, WRITING CYPHERS, AND WPA WORK

I am the junior WPA (jWPA) at a midsize Northeastern urban
historically black university, otherwise referred to as an HBCU.
Within our writing program, we employ a variety of full-time lec-
turers, who range from creative writers to literary scholars, compositionists, and historians. The bulk of my work revolves around
negotiating the institutional culture of the university, the student
culture shaping many of the students' attitudes and dispositions,
and the eclectic cosmopolitan (or Afropolitan depending on whom
you talk to) culture of the city that encapsulates the university and
influences our visions of language and culture. In 2015, we began

a curricular redesign that sought to merge a WAW approach with an emphasis on race and culture. The thinking behind this was to maintain the cultural studies and social justice emphasis that has informed the program identity for decades, while updating and facilitating the ways teachers and students thought and talked about composition studies together. Because of our large black and minority populations (which make up about 90 percent of the student population), we've begun to think significantly about the role of race in writing instruction.

WAW develops out of the writing studies movement, which focuses on the intellectual and cultural work that frames and produces writing. In "Writing Studies as a Mode of Inquiry," Susan Miller suggested we think of writing studies as a disciplinary project. In doing so, we might make writing studies a way of placing textual analysis at the center of the field of rhetoric and composition and avoid negative as well as narrow interpretations of composition studies as the "mere" teaching of writing skills (42). For Miller, rhetoric and composition studies benefit from the examination and teaching of texts that place writing histories within contexts that help explain "who, to what ends, and, especially, how people have written and do write" (52). For Miller, writing studies is a way of providing rhetoric and composition studies a subject, but also, more ambitiously, functions as a way of expanding the way we think about and discuss writing as a subject. With Miller, the objective is to make the moves, questions, and traditions connected to writing more visible and transparent for students, to demystify the enterprise of composition studies, and to place researched knowledge at its center.

More recent scholarship in writing studies relies on the theme of WAW to describe the core tenets of composition studies. A central practice of such an approach requires students to read articles related to threshold concepts in the field written by notable scholars. By focusing on facilitating a historical consciousness about rhetoric and composition among students, writing studies has largely become associated with an approach toward teaching writing that wrests control about expertise from a crisis-driven public. As

Elizabeth Wardle and Doug Downs explain, the WAW approach centers the teaching of writing on conversations and scholarship that shape the study and application of rhetoric and composition (iv–vi). In their textbook *Writing about Writing: A College Reader* they explain, "it made far more sense to us to have students really engage with writing in the writing course; the best way to do this, we decided, was to adopt a 'writing about writing' approach, introducing students directly to what writing researchers have learned about writing and challenging them to respond by writing and by doing research of their own" (v). This recentering was in response to the feeling that composition courses were becoming less about the concepts of writing and more about special themes and topics. To them, this lack of "focus" contributed to the public loss of confidence in contemporary writing instruction.

While Wardle and Downs's textbook provides a useful explanation of the WAW and its focus on threshold concepts, the book itself tends to avoid cultural rhetoric, and specifically African American rhetorical theory, as a framing resource. Authors such as Malcolm X, Sherman Alexie, Jabari Mahiri, and Soraya Sablo pepper the reading selections for the text, but the threshold concepts used to organize the book remain fairly general in their discussion of discourse communities, technology, and rhetoric. Each section provides a list of writings around one of these concepts, but none of the pieces provide a conversation that introduces students to concepts such as signifyin or counternarratives as valuable rhetorical concepts for writers. From my perspective WAW only gains life through complexity and variation. By this I mean that without a comparative understanding of valuable concepts that exist in other traditions students are diminished as rhetorical power players, as writers, thinkers, and actors capable of drawing on and understanding the best of the traditions in which they find their own style, language, or voice. As proponents of cultural rhetoric might argue, the best way to value and understand ethnic and cultural rhetorical traditions is to read and work with them not as alternative categories or subcategories of rhetoric, but as meaningful contributions to how we might think about and discuss writing with teachers and students, and to how we design our writing programs.

To be clear, *Writing about Writing: A College Reader* is a laudable undertaking, and in some ways an apt extension of what Miller attempted to outline in her case for writing studies. My current impression though is that Miller's interest in histories of unique writings, of unique textual case studies, is asking compositionists not just to think differently about the concepts taught in writing courses or to simply take control of writing from an anxious public, but also to rethink what histories and positions about writing we provide to students. What might it mean for students to understand their literacies and creative practices as part of a larger writing tradition? And what might it mean to position these writing traditions as vital to addressing the inequality and discrimination that exist across a number of institutions and within the broader world? For students at Howard, many of whom come to the university seeking an education and an experience that value the complexity of a diasporic blackness, such an attention to conversations about writing and culture can be eye-opening. Our goal as a program is to frame writing for these students as a transcultural process that requires them to assume linguistic and cultural pluralism as a material reality always shaping how they view any rhetorical situation they enter.

Within this context, cyphers become an interesting way of thinking about writing traditions with students, because cyphers are organic circles of interaction separate from formal writing. From a hip-hop studies perspective, cyphers represent an ongoing conversation about the composing process that is linked directly to the compositions and ideas shared within each cypher. For my purposes, cyphers provide a mode of thinking and interacting that serves an inventional and creative function, that over time fosters community and inspires careful dialogue. H. Samy Alim describes the cypher as a circle of interaction in which participants compete and challenge one another to sharpen their skills and share ideas in the "spirit of both teaching and learning" (2). The beauty for him is that the cypher values spontaneity and ongoing knowledge production in ways that are fruitful for language users and critical writers. In *Hip Hop Underground: The Integrity and Ethics of Racial Identification*, Anthony Kwame Harrison also notes that cyphers often birth from impromptu encounters that call forth participants who have a perspective to share; by its very nature the cypher is a critical call-and-response practice central to creating a writing community (3). Thus, with respect to writing programs, one might come to see cyphers as circles of deliberation necessary for particular conversations about writing to occur. Each cypher produces a new rhetorical situation and audience that individuals may use to revise and better prepare their positions for newer audiences and different circumstances.

However, cyphers also provide a way for us to think through conversations facilitated among teachers of writing. Because the focus of the cypher is about learning through difference, the structure of the cypher becomes an invitation for deliberating about the performance and possibilities of writing that exist within different cultures or across difference spaces. It is an invitation to think with our fellow teachers about composing voices, composing viewpoints, and rethinking what quality means. In "Deeper than Rap: Expanding Conceptions of Hip-Hop Culture and Pedagogy in the English Language Classroom," H. Bernard Hall asserts that we can benefit from a more expansive view of hip-hop, one that moves beyond a focus on musical content and focuses on the possibilities hip-hop provides our curricular and pedagogical interests (344). As Hall notes, teachers might benefit just as much from deep consideration of the aesthetic and rhetorical practices of hip-hop such as the cypher and the freestyle as they would from analysis of hip-hop lyrics (345). Yet the idea of the "cypher" provides a type of structure for sharpening the way writing traditions are understood, as well. As Hall himself notes, the cypher deployed as a hip-hop literate practice asks one to "reconceptualiz[e] hegemonic notions of knowledge and the teacher-student relationship" (346). While writing instructors are positioned as experts in their own right, their decisions about instruction are viewed as collective and context-driven. Instructors are asked to make critical decisions about what examples for their lessons to share and what readings to assign. Moreover, most writing instructors are the first people to have conversations with students about what it means to write within a university space shaping their perspective on academic writing, likely for the long term.

Furthermore, the cypher can be used to organize a number of elements of a writing program. Theories of the cypher provide a way of thinking about teacher training in ways that do not overtax writing faculty, and instead asks them to rethink writing instruction and curricular goals with an eye toward student performances. At my university, writing faculty often teach four classes a semester on annual contracts, and supplement these positions with more teaching elsewhere. Moreover, many of the faculty are trained in fields such as literature and creative writing, with little to no formal training in rhetoric or composition beyond the training sessions required by our program. Thus, what we have tried to do in terms of professional development is to organize discussions about writing around topics that put pressure on the readings, assignments, and approaches deemed relevant to students.

When placed within a writing program, then, the cypher promotes a different way of understanding authorship, arrangement, and rhetorical knowledge that, as James Peterson notes, derives from a rich tradition of African American textual production that converges within underground spaces and tends to privilege a nonlinear orientation toward sharing one's work (85). Thus, the textual products composed and circulated among hip-hop communities highlight one way I reimagine the types of writing that students complete in our program. My purpose is to place instructors and myself in positions to listen and learn through shared debate about the immediate value of the concepts, practices, and assumptions that animate our students. For our program at Howard, the cypher becomes a way of recognizing the differences—in opinions, values, ethnicities, professional training—that exist among our writing faculty and asking them to begin to engage them. Obviously, differences in professional training and teaching approaches will continue to influence our writing instructors, but the main push is for them to begin to consider imaginative writing, invention, and delivery with an eye toward the cultural identities and values that animate student discourse and informs the ways that they enter and exit various forms of language.

VISIONS AND CYPHERS AT THE MODERN HBCU

An outcome of our curricular redesign was the publication of the textbook *Visions and Cyphers*. The book was designed around the idea of engaging students in multiple cyphers around issues central to composition studies. Part of our goal was to frame these issues for students as unfinished and part of ongoing conversations about the way academic writing is viewed by teachers and administrators, and to explore the ways they may choose to view writing whether academic or nonacademic.

The textbook was designed in units, or what we characterized as cyphers, that place essays in conversation to enable the student to better reflect on the field of composition studies and to think critically about what writing in various genres entails. However, unlike some traditional writing texts, this textbook presses for this awareness through a series of readings, reflective questions, and reflective assignments that place the study and theorizing of composition at its center. Thus, unlike in other writing courses, students are encouraged to think critically about prescribed rules, about the function and structure of academic writings, about definitions of plagiarism, and about differing definitions of research, evidence, and identity. Debate about these topics, no matter how ambiguous some of them may seem, is encouraged, explored, and rewarded. In Wardle and Downs's *Writing about Writing,* the structure of the text and the sequence of concepts place an emphasis on concepts central to how people make meaning through the writing process. They introduce students to concepts such as literacy, mediation, rhetoric, process analysis, and multimodality through a reflective frame that asks students to question as they observe the complex writing about the subject of writing. Our approach to *Visions and Cyphers* also encourages students to observe complex conversations about writing as they learn as well, but with an emphasis on asking them to think about how learning and writing spring forth from a variety of traditions, and how these traditions shape the rhetorical choices available to writers in a given situation. Our text also asks them to question the structure of how writing is presented to them within formal academic spaces, sometimes intentionally as a way to interrupt or obstruct the joys they might find in nontraditional forms of intellectual writing.

The opening cypher includes Jacqueline Jones Royster's "When the First Voice You Hear Is Not Your Own," Jabari Mahiri and Soraya Sablo's "Writing for Their Lives: The Non-School Literacy of California's Urban African American Youth," Keith Gilyard's "Literacy Identity, Imagination, and Flight," and Shirley Logan's "Why College English." These essays were organized to help students consider the ways that race and literacy inform how one values the multiple literacies afforded them. In particular, it is assumed that writing is simultaneously a personal and a formal endeavor, and one that shapes how writing can be valued beyond a rather simplistic academic grading system that categorizes without empathy or vision. As Gerald Graff notes, the in-school structure is such that students are usually socialized to compartmentalize and omit contradictions in information or approaches. At the heart of what I am suggesting about the ways we cultivate critical reading practices among teachers and students is an assumption of value in the embodied experiences and cultural competencies motivating students and shaping a continuous dialogue.

Instructors and students work to develop their own dispositions regarding race and literacy as well as trying to cultivate a clear understanding of the different objectives that academic writing holds for them and the objectives for writing they may have for themselves. Marcyliena Morgan notes that language is intricately tied to identity, aesthetics, morality, and epistemology. For this reason, learning to be proficient in certain cultural situations requires extensive and textured language socialization. Morgan proposes the concept of social face as a way of acknowledging the performative nature of language and identity. Individuals are always communicating within and across various discourse communities (38–39). As she notes, language diversity does not present the type of boundaries normally assumed; people often find a way to communicate and interact with those different from them when necessary to function socially.

Logan's essay in particular asks students to question the value of their own composition training for their expressive goals and their critical understanding of public discourse. As Logan notes, "my overriding concern, then, is that we continue to decenter, not remove, concepts that limit our understanding of college English to primarily the study of words, the study of correctness, and the study of Eurocentric texts and that we teach students of college English more intentionally how to analyze and deploy language and images in ways that better prepare for meaningful civic engagement." The idea of expanding through cultural awareness is centrally themed in my classes and the program itself through the use of the cypher.

CYPHERING ABOUT WHITENESS AT HBCUS

Cyphers provide added value to WPA work well beyond simply how they help structure curriculum and classroom instruction. When I think of cyphers and WPA work, I also think about how cyphers open up spaces to reflect, challenge, and question the whiteness that often structures the stories we tell about writing and writing traditions within our writing programs. Although HBCUs are predominantly black institutions, they are far from immune to the ideological work of whiteness and its influence. As noted elsewhere, HBCUs tend to struggle with deeply entrenched attitudes about correctness and standardized speech (Spencer-Maor and Randolph 179). These attitudes rely on assumptions about "appropriateness" and "conventions" that are constructed in opposition to difference or nonwhiteness. In "Reading 'Whiteness' in English Studies," Timothy Barnett situates whiteness as an idealized set of discursive practices imbued with objective authority that does not disclose its historical or political connections to institutions and groups of people invested in normalizing particular power relations (13). For Barnett, whiteness works to render itself invisible in ways that affirm particular practices as "the standard." These practices work to further entrench attitudes about writing and writing instruction by facilitating a belief system that normalizes assumptions about literacy, language, and writing in ways that position linguistic or stylistic differences as of lesser value than standardized writing conventions or language.

Cyphers provide a means of complicating the daily narratives circulated about language, race, and difference among select groups of people willing to engage in ongoing and evolving discussions of writing and language. Thus, I am enamored with the difficult work Aja Martinez describes in "A Plea for Critical Race Theory Counterstory: Stock Story versus Counterstory Dialogues Concerning Alejandra's 'Fit' in the Academy." The article attempts to describe an exigence and formalize a counterstory methodology for composition studies in part because of the way many narratives that circulate in composition studies normalize a type of whiteness that works against the epistemologies and practices students of color bring with them to the classroom. What might it mean to develop cyphers as WPA concepts designed to facilitate discussions or debates around counterstories deployed against existing assumptions about language or race within composition?

In *More Beautiful and More Terrible: The Embrace and Transcendence of Racial Inequality in the United States* Imani Perry argues that narratives are "fundamental to the way we as humans structure our lives and operate within the world as individuals and members of communities. The use of parable, metonym, and metaphor allow[s] us to project a given story into new contexts" (44). For Perry, racial narratives often oscillate between negative and positive in a variety of ways that require interrogation of competing narratives. As Perry notes, there is a public narrative about inner-city public education that often shifts the blame of failing schools toward lack of motivation and low expectations by students and parents in the community. Yet, equally vibrant, according to Perry, are narratives of students like those in the Young People's Project in Baltimore who protest the inadequate funding and availability of advanced courses and expert teachers for their school system (61).

As these narratives circulate among group formations through shared dialogue and shared cultural values, cyphers represent ways of reimagining these formations and the ways narratives move among and across cyphers to shape interactions. Given that difference shapes the reality most of us must experience, whether the difference is gendered, racialized, cultural, regional, economic, or political, any engagement with difference requires that individuals come to interrogate the types of narratives about writing and culture that have been valued as "standard" and important and the types that have been seen as "other" or nonstandard and devalued in the writing classroom. In this way cyphers provide a structure for the type of communities around writing vital to expanding the embrace of various writing traditions. Not too long ago, I was asked to have a talk with a writing instructor who made a few comments to her class about the high attrition rates of black college students and the poor performance of black students on standardized tests. As was no surprise to me, such comments drew several angry rebuttals from her first-year students, many of whom were black and anxious about their own positions as new students, and many of whom were valedictorians or high-achieving students. Their anxieties were exacerbated by the fact that the instructor, who was of mixed ethnic lineage, racially identified herself as white and European through comments she made to the students. Although the writing instructor did not mean for her comments to offend, that mattered little to the students. However insensitive one might perceive the comments to be, it was the response to the students' attempts to rebut the claims that drew much of their ire. Using themselves as counterarguments to the national narrative about black school achievement, many of the students attempted to argue that the narrative the instructor presented to them was flawed. But they believed that their rebuttals were summarily dismissed.

After several students made verbal complaints, I invited the instructor to meet and discuss the students' feelings on the matter, but our meeting was cut short as the instructor took offense at how the students framed the debate in their complaints. My attempts to discuss the matter were met with disbelief, outrage, and an angry exit from my office. I was subsequently accused by the instructor of (1) siding with the students without hearing the instructor's side of the story and (2) jeopardizing the instructor's livelihood. It took another meeting with the department chair and the assistant dean of the college before the instructor would admit to misreading the situation. As I would explain in the meeting with the department chair and assistant dean, the initial meeting with the instructor was only to get her perspective on the events and to discuss the complexity of the narrative she was sharing with the students. The instructor would eventually give credence to the students' feelings, and no further administrative action would be taken, but the incident would highlight how damaging it is to avoid discussions of race.

I fully understand the power dynamics of the incident and the ways my initial interaction was misinterpreted. The instructor was anxious, and rightly so. Writing faculty at my institution are reappointed annually based in part on my recommendation. This power, which the instructor admitted later was heightened by my black male body and quiet demeanor, raised her anxiety. The university, like many HBCUs, comprises a broad spectrum of students. From high-achieving students who come to the university speaking three languages to students who might academically underperform or might be on probation after serving time in jail and being given a second chance. Had the instructor not been anxious, and had we had a chance to talk in depth about the scenario, I would have mentioned that the destructive potential of the narratives she shared outweighed the probative and informative value of the information she shared with the students. As Perry describes, "racial narratives are stories that are told about members of racial groups in daily conversations, in print, through the broadcast and new media, in literature, and in child rearing," as a way of learning about those groups (44). As I did tell the instructor, having known her for some time, I understood her comments were not malicious, but that all instruction takes place within contexts and among particular audiences, which requires recognition and the flexibility to shift or adjust teaching practices.

As other colleagues at other HBCUs have shared with me, these occurrences are not infrequent. The institution of higher education tends to normalize whiteness in writing instruction, at times intentionally and at times unintentionally, and often at great and violent expense to students of color. As Craig and Perryman-Clark mentioned, such a gaze questions the ethical nature of a WPA of color and assumes that because one is a person of color and speaking on behalf of a student of color that his or her interests are necessarily aligned against the instructor and with the student (21). My department chair was instrumental in resolving the situation, but I cannot help wondering, given the frequency of these occurrences shared by colleagues at other HBCUs, how WPAs at HBCUs might better facilitate conversations about critical race work advocated by several scholars in the field (see Holmes; Campbell; Banks; Kynard, *Vernacular*.) In our department writing retreats we have often talked about culture as an important factor in the types of readings and assignments provided to students. Yet such work becomes paramount for teachers working within these spaces as they provide a shift for the broader narrative of college composition.

If we push the analysis a little further, we could argue that cyphers about race and writing provide a unique space to think through the public narratives about students of color and academic success that are often shared and recited regarding education. These cyphers provide a way to discuss narratives about our students in productive ways, as well as what practices gathered student interest and for what reason. Often, I find this a productive ground from which to begin conversations about literacy acquisition and the work we believe our assignments achieve. For many teachers within our program, there is a shared belief that we are training students to get corporate jobs that will require pages of expository writing every week. Of course, I am being facetious, but through our cyphers and discussions it became possible for me to address assumptions about the disadvantages teachers believed students of color experienced simply because of their race or ethnicity. This allowed me to shift our conversations about assignments toward a focus on developing critical thinkers by assessing the rhetorical decisions students make when attempting to solve a problem and move away from an overemphasis on correctness as the dynamic element of writing that would win them the imagined jobs awaiting them.

Other cyphers formed in this endeavor include sharing topics discussed over an internal group email listserv as well as the informal cyphers that form within shared office spaces and hallways.

The organic flow of these practices allows for the conversation to remain ongoing yet guided by me and others who wish to share their thinking about composition. I am arguing, then, that if we are to continue to put pressure on the public narratives shaping our views of students, there must be a concerted effort to construct a writing program that moves beyond blame and shame, focusing rather on productive ways of questioning ourselves regarding the public narratives about student identities that we often take for granted.

ERROR, DEFICIT ATTITUDES, AND ALTERNATE LINGUISTIC EPISTEMOLOGIES

The problem of microaggressions at HBCUs remains separate from but related to deficit attitudes that remain prevalent in these spaces. In many instances, students simply adjust to these attitudes and negotiate instructors or assignments through a variety of strategies. As Elaine Richardson points out, "African American students train themselves to deal with the inequality of the educational experience and general societal conflicts. One option for school success for African American students lies in enduring the system and avoiding or masking vernacular literacies" (16). Students learn to adjust their behavior or arguments to align with their instructors as a survival strategy, and while this is common in many higher education institutions it takes on a different level of complexity at HBCUs, specifically with regard to shifting instructor attitudes about assignments and assessment.

Deficit attitudes, specifically within an HBCU setting, provide a complex wrinkle in WPA work as these attitudes often emerge in moments of tension exacerbated by the complexity of student writing. James Slevin astutely argued that the work of composition is not in the teaching of writing but in the ways one comes to understand the difficulty of writing (19). For Slevin, student writing presents a space to examine the textual moves writers make as well as writing's relevance to their literate and social lives (21). Probably the most persistent examples of microaggressions toward students of color that occur in our writing program, on the other hand, derive from a preoccupation with student language and "lack." I use lack to describe not just a belief in student deficits that shape how writing is managed, taught, and measured, but a fundamental inability to see student writing as anything more than a purely functional type of literacy practice. I refer to this sometimes as the disbelief approach. That is, a fundamental commitment to disbelief in student competence and labor surrounding their written responses to complex social phenomena. A common refrain that I've heard from countless instructors proposes that "students need to learn to write a sentence before they can compose an essay." In some ways I interpret this statement to mean "we do not trust you to tell your own stories, and we do not trust that your stories will not expose the very differences we seek to mollify and smooth over through instruction." While I do not see such positions as malicious attempts to silence students, such overt concern about students' lack of knowledge regarding the basic structures of sentences or knowledge of pronoun and antecedent agreement belies a type of microaggression persistent within many writing programs. Laura Greenfield notes that such overt concerns about correctness are often illustrated through examples about student speech, or what students can articulate about the rules of language, without much consideration of the incongruence between oral and written language (40). She uses such incongruence to point out that the emphasis on correctness stems less from nuanced considerations of written language and its possibilities, and more from a legacy of hyperpolicing black and other students of color (34–35).

Though not the majority in my WPA experience, I have definitely had a number of instructors, some at conferences, some from other disciplines, and some working within my own writing program, describe in passionate detail the need for skill-and-drill lessons for students given their horrible grasp of grammatical rules and "the basic components of a sentence." Ironically, many of these same instructors develop the most detailed and innovative assignments for writing once they move beyond this fascination with correctness. This push-pull attitude around language remains prominent among broader discussions of Black English use (see

Alim and Smitherman, *Articulate while Black*). Yet this type of deficit thinking remains ever present, even after decades of scholarship highlighting its questionable history and detrimental effects.

In the fall of 2013, I invited Bonnie Williams-Farrier to hold a short workshop on African American modes of discourse and ways to employ these modes in formal writing instruction. The goal was to introduce instructors to alternate ways of thinking about language and writing that diverge from the traditional modes of discourse. As Williams-Farrier noted, signifying, rhythm, sounding, repetition, chiasmus, and other modes provided ways of thinking about the choices that black writers make not as errors, but as rhetorical choices deriving from an alternate epistemic-knowledge base. Williams-Farrier would elaborate on the workshop provided to our program in an article later published in the journal *Meridians*, "Signifying, Narrativizing, and Repetition: Radical Approaches to Theorizing African American Language." The strength of her work for my purposes was couched in her elaboration on the African American verbal tradition (AVT), or what she frames as the rhetorical strategies of African American discourse that remain central to understanding many of the moves of African American writers. As she notes, "AVT is a small portion of a large African American rhetorical tradition that exceeds the verbal to include non-verbal and written communication" (220). The larger claims of the article highlight the way students' use of nonstandardized English speech varieties have been used to stigmatize students and label them as deficient, whether intentionally or unintentionally, before they even arrived in the classroom (223). Workshops such as Williams-Farrier's provide a type of counterstory to the prevailing deficit narrative that surrounds the language of students of color. These counterstories put pressure on instructors to reflect and adapt their teaching. Of particular value to our cyphers was Williams-Farrier's discussion of comparative rhetorical approaches to teaching writing that acknowledged non-Western rhetorical strategies as valid and useful in composing. I think we lose something if we view or present to students WAW as a unitary tradition that fits neatly into certain categories of inquiry, but do not also highlight the way the study and act of writing is always informed by specific cultures and specific histories. For my purposes, it is important for students to understand the complex conversations around what writing is and how it is taught, but those conversations differ according to which traditions are drawn on as resources. Following Williams-Farrier's presentation several cyphers about language and African American writing practices developed at later writing retreats and professional development workshops. Important to me was that ideas about correctness and language difference would become powerful points of discussion moving forward.

Many instructors would still hold fast to their assertions that these students needed grammatical training and familiarity with sentence-styling. As I would share with them, I did not disagree that all students can use guided practice with grammar, style, and mechanics, but that these things were largely ineffective if taught outside of the context and purpose of a given student's writing. While I hesitate to describe our workshop as a cypher, the discussion around this topic allowed instructors to discuss and theorize about language and race in ways that made them stakeholders in the success of the program. It asked them to take a macrolevel view of the lessons and ideas about writing they provided students.

TABLES AND SEATS: FINAL THOUGHTS

As we rethink the role of hip-hop and other cultural rhetorics in theorizing WPA work at HBCUs and other like-kind institutions, it becomes imperative to rethink the stories that circulate through our programs regarding the students these programs serve. The idea of the cypher becomes valuable as a way to engage instructors not formally trained in composition in conversations about race, language, and writing that often unsettle the silence surrounding such topics. Given this reality, it becomes important to begin to exhaust newer or different ways of thinking through WPA work in the spaces that exist. To that extent, I am curious about what other practices can be developed from alternative epistemologies about discourse that can be useful in thinking through the training and development of writing instructors in these spaces.

I am reminded of bell hooks's comments in *Teaching Community* that antiracist work is an ongoing endeavor designed to help all of us better navigate the diverse communities that exist within our democracy (80). We can never fully protect ourselves from racist assaults "in a world that is not yet anti-racist but incredibly diverse" (80), but can learn from one another in ways that foster newer conceptions of community, and of the ways we learn. Part of this growth is steeped in the stories we share, and the way we use those stories to continually challenge our thinking.

WORKS CITED

Adler-Kassner, Linda, and Elizabeth Wardle, editors. *Naming What We Know: Threshold Concepts of Writing Studies.* Utah State UP, 2015.

Alim, H. Samy. *Roc the Mic Right: The Language of Hip Hop Culture.* Routledge, 2006.

Alim, H. Samy, and Geneva Smitherman. *Articulate while Black: Barack Obama, Language, and Race in the U.S.* Oxford UP, 2012.

Alvarez, Steven. "Brokering the Immigrant Bargain: Second-Generation Immigrant Youth Negotiating Transnational Orientations to Literacy." *Literacy in Composition Studies*, vol. 3, no. 3, Oct. 2015, pp. 25–47.

Banks, Adam J. *Digital Griots: African American Rhetoric in a Multimedia Age.* Southern Illinois UP, 2011.

Barnett, Timothy. "Reading 'Whiteness' in English Studies." *College English*, vol. 63, no. 1, Sep. 2000, pp. 9–37.

Campbell, Kermit E. *Gettin' Our Groove On: Rhetoric, Language, and Literacy for the Hip Hop Generation.* Wayne State UP, 2005.

Craig, Collin Lamont, and Staci M. Perryman-Clark. "Troubling the Boundaries Revisited: Moving towards Change as Things Stay the Same." *Writing Program Administration*, vol. 39, no.2, Spring 2016, pp 20–26.

Gold, David. *Rhetoric at the Margins: Revising the History of Writing Instruction in American Colleges, 1873–1947.* Southern Illinois UP, 2008.

Graff, Gerald. "Hidden Intellectualism." *Pedagogy,* vol. 1, issue 1, Winter 2001, pp. 21–36.

Green, David F., Jr. "Expanding the Dialogue on Writing Assessment at HBCUs: Foundational Assessment Concepts and Legacies of Historically Black Colleges and Universities." *College English,* vol. 79, no. 2. Nov. 2016, pp. 152–73.

———. *Visions and Cyphers: Explorations of Literacy, Discourse, and Black Writing Experiences.* Imprint Editions, 2016.

Greenfield, Laura. "The 'Standard English' Fairy Tale: A Rhetorical Analysis of Racist Pedagogies and Commonplace Assumptions about Language Diversity." *Writing Centers and the New Racism: A Call for Sustainable Dialogue and Change,* edited by Greenfield and Karen Rowan, Utah State UP, 2011, pp. 33–60.

Hall, H. Bernard. "Deeper Than Rap: Expanding Conceptions of Hip-Hop Culture and Pedagogy in the English Language Arts Classroom." *Research in the Teaching of English,* vol. 51, no. 3, Feb. 2017, pp. 341–50.

Harrison, Anthony Kwame. *Hip Hop Underground: The Integrity and Ethics of Racial Identification.* Temple UP, 2009.

Holmes, David. "Fighting Back by Writing Black: Beyond Racially Reductive Composition Theory." *Race, Rhetoric, and Composition,* edited by Keith Gilyard, Boynton/Cook, 1999, pp.53–66.

hooks, bell. *Teaching Community: A Pedagogy of Hope.* Routledge, 2003.

Knowles, Solange. "F.U.B.U." *A Seat at the Table,* Saint Records and Columbia Records, 2016.

Kynard, Carmen. "Teaching while Black: Witnessing and Countering Disciplinary Whiteness, Racial Violence, and University Race-Management." *Literacy in Composition Studies,* vol. 3, no.1, Mar. 2015, pp. 1–20.

———. *Vernacular Insurrections: Race, Black Protest, and the New Century in Composition-Literacies Studies.* SUNY P, 2013.

Kynard, Carmen, and Robert Eddy. "Toward a New Critical Framework: Color-Conscious Political Morality and Pedagogy at Historically Black and Historically White Colleges and Universities." *College Composition and Communication,* vol. 61, no. 1, Sept. 2009, pp. W24–W44.

Martinez, Aja Y. "A Plea for Critical Race Theory Counterstory: Stock Story versus Counterstory Dialogues Concerning Alejandra's 'Fit' in the Academy." *Composition Studies*, vol. 42, no. 2, Fall 2014, pp. 33–55.

Miller, Susan. "Writing Studies as a Mode of Inquiry." *Rhetoric and Composition as Intellectual Work*, edited by Gary A. Olson, Southern Illinois UP, 2002, pp. 41–54.

Morgan, Marcyliena. *Language, Discourse and Power in African American Culture.* Cambridge UP, 2002.

Perry, Imani. *More Beautiful and More Terrible: The Embrace and Transcendence of Racial Inequality in the United States.* New York UP, 2011.

Peterson, James Braxton. *The Hip-Hop Underground and African American Culture: Beneath the Surface.* Palgrave Macmillan, 2014.

Richardson, Elaine. *African American Literacies.* Routledge, 2003.

Royster, Jacqueline Jones. "When the First Voice You Hear Is Not Your Own." *College Composition and Communication*, vol. 47, no. 1, Feb. 1996, pp. 29–40.

Slevin, James F. *Introducing English: Essays in the Intellectual Work of Composition.* U of Pittsburgh P, 2001.

Spencer-Maor, Faye, and Robert E. Randolph Jr. "Shifting the Talk: Writing Studies, Rhetoric, and Feminism at HBCUs." *Composition Studies*, vol. 44, no. 2, Fall 2016, pp. 179–82.

Wardle, Elizabeth, and Doug Downs. "Preface for Instructors." *Writing about Writing: A College Reader,* edited by Wardle and Downs, 2nd ed., Bedford/St. Martin's, 2014, pp. v–xii.

Williams-Farrier, Bonnie J. "Signifying, Narrativizing, and Repetition: Radical Approaches to Theorizing African American Language." *Meridians: Feminism, Race, Transnationalism*, vol. 15, no. 1, 2016, pp. 218–42.

Zebroski, James T. "Disciplinary Narratives 1980–2000: A Cultural Rhetoric Approach." *Narrative Acts: Rhetoric, Race and Identity, Knowledge,* edited by Debra Journet, Beth A. Boehm, and Cynthia E. Britt, Hampton Press, 2011, pp. 21–36.

4

Forfeiting Privilege for the Cause of Social Justice: Listening to Black WPAs and WPAs of Color Define the Work of White Allyship

Scott Wible

> It is our allies . . . who can be vital for navigating conflicts and survival of WPAs of color, especially microaggressive behaviors that seek to undermine the ethos, power, and authority of WPAs of color. . . . [W]hite faculty must consider how much of their own privilege they are willing to forfeit for the cause of social justice.
>
> —Collin Lamont Craig and Staci M. Perryman-Clark, "Troubling the Boundaries Revisited"

From their 2011 and 2016 *WPA* articles "Troubling the Boundaries" and "Troubling the Boundaries Revisited" to this present collection, Collin Craig and Staci Perryman-Clark have exposed the "interlocking discourses of [racial and gender] oppression" and resulting "status quo of power relations" within writing program administration work at their local institutions as well as within the wider discipline ("Troubling the Boundaries" 55). They have narrated their experiences locally and nationally to carry out work as WPAs—and to find support from colleagues for that work—within institutions and writing programs where racist logics motivate the "policing of black bodies, black labor, and black intellectual work" (ch. 1, this volume, p. 00) and, in turn, "undermine the ethos, power, and authority of WPAs of color" ("Troubling the Boundaries Revisited" 22). Several other scholarly projects have continued this work, heightening our awareness of racial discrimination in

writing programs and deepening our understanding of how normative assumptions about race, ethnicity, and language shape writing
program administration's disciplinary identity—projects including
the formation of a People of Color Caucus within the Council of
Writing Program Administrators (CWPA); a symposium on race
and writing program administration in the *WPA Journal;* Genevieve García de Müeller and Iris Ruiz's CCCC Research Initiative–
funded study of race and WPA work, which has resulted in part
in their 2017 *WPA* article "Race, Silence, and Writing Program
Administration: A Qualitative Study of U.S. College Writing Programs"; Asao B. Inoue's plenary address at the 2016 CWPA Conference titled "Racism in Writing Programs and the CWPA"; and
efforts by WPA-GO, the graduate organization within CWPA, to
facilitate roundtable discussions at CCCC and CWPA conferences
about race, diversity, and social justice in graduate education and
training. But as Craig and Perryman-Clark make clear in the epi-
graph above, from their 2016 essay "Troubling the Boundaries Revisited," the responsibility for creating an equitable, diverse discipline does not rest solely on the shoulders of black WPAs and other
WPAs of color. White WPAs and writing studies scholars, if they
truly, deeply care about creating socially just working and learning
experiences not only for their black colleagues and students but also
for themselves, must "work alongside" black WPAs "in a spirit of
equity and diversity" ("Troubling the Boundaries" 54–55).

This essay, then, explores the practice of white allyship in writing program administration, analyzing specific contexts in which
white WPAs can work alongside black WPAs and WPAs of color to
support their research and administrative work, to promote a new
vision of the field grounded in antiracist principles, and to carry out
this vision in daily practice within our major professional organizations and our local institutions. My approach to researching and
writing this article has been informed by Jacqueline Jones Royster's
call in her 1995 CCCC Chair's Address, "When the First Voice You
Hear Is Not Your Own." Here Royster argues that those in historically privileged positions need to learn how to listen when working
with and on issues of racial difference:

How can we teach, engage in research, write about, and talk across boundaries with others, instead of for, about, and around them? My experiences tell me that we need to do more than just talk and talk back. I believe that in this model we miss a critical moment. We need to talk, yes, and to talk back, yes, but when do we listen? How do we listen? How do we demonstrate that we honor and respect the person talking and what that person is saying, or what the person might say if we valued someone other than ourselves having a turn to speak? How do we translate listening into language and action, into the creation of an appropriate response? How do we really "talk back" rather than talk also? The goal is not, "You talk, I talk." The goal is better practices so that we can exchange perspectives, negotiate meaning, and create understanding with the intent of being in a good position to cooperate, when, like now, cooperation is absolutely necessary. (38)

This chapter, then, has taken shape through acts of listening to black WPAs and WPAs of color, and it aims to help white WPAs begin to translate this listening into action. Specifically, this essay draws on ten hourlong interviews with WPAs, including seven black WPAs and WPAs of color and three white WPAs who had been identified as allies by some of the WPAs of color I interviewed. Six of the WPAs of color are tenure-track assistant professors, and the seventh is a writing program lecturer with an extensive research and publishing record, including a published monograph and grant-funded projects focused on WPA issues. The black WPAs and WPAs of color work at a range of institutions:

- a medium-sized, higher research activity (Carnegie R2), private Historically Black College [or] University (HBCU) in the Northeast
- a large, higher research activity (Carnegie R2), public university in the Southeast
- a medium-sized, higher research activity (Carnegie R2), public HBCU in the Southeast

- a large, moderate research activity (Carnegie R3), public Hispanic Serving Institution (HSI) in the Southwest
- a medium-sized, higher research activity (Carnegie R2), public HSI in the West
- a large, highest research activity (Carnegie R1), private university in the Northeast
- and a large, higher research activity (Carnegie R2), public university in the Northeast

Interview questions prompted these scholars to describe their previous and current WPA activities and their professional aspirations; to narrate experiences that illustrate how race and ethnicity has affected their work as WPAs; and to offer a working definition of "ally" and any examples of how they have been supported by white allies or how they have worked or attempted to act as allies for black colleagues or graduate students. While these general topics were addressed in each interview, interview questions were not followed as a script; rather, the interviews took the form of conversation, with follow-up questions asked to prompt more details and examples. Even as the interviews took this conversational shape, however, I was guided throughout by Royster's question: "How do we demonstrate that we honor and respect the person talking and what that person is saying, or what the person might say if we valued someone other than ourselves having a turn to speak?" This perspective also informed my approach to analyzing the interview data and drafting the essay, as well. Heeding Royster's warning that "[t]he goal is not, 'You talk, I talk,'" I have tried to foreground the voices of the black WPAs and WPAs of color in this essay more than my own. Toward that end, two to three extended quotations from these interviews open and focus each major section in the body of this essay. While I do provide my own reflective responses to these longer interview passages, I do so as a way to show my own attempts to "create understanding" (Royster 38). I keep my own reflective sections brief, however, in the spirit of—to paraphrase Royster—valuing someone other than yet another white male WPA having a turn to speak.

"GIVE SOMETHING UP, PUT SOMETHING ON THE LINE": EXAMINING WHITE PRIVILEGE IN WPAS' EDUCATIONAL AND PROFESSIONAL EXPERIENCE

An ally is someone who believes a person of color and doesn't try to rationalize away the person's experiences and perceptions of racism. . . . There are too many faculty who say "go away" rather than engaging and figuring it out. For people of color, it's hard work, every single day. It's hard work, and we can't take a single day off. It's constant work—day after day after day. There have been many instances of colleagues who could have gained my confidence, showed me what they do when they have an opportunity to support and advocate for a person of color, but they just go away when difficulty appears.

White allies have an understanding of how institutions reproduce racism and acknowledge the added level of vulnerability that pretenure scholars of color experience when they also hold an administrative position. . . . As a pretenure scholar and assistant WPA, I managed and taught in the writing programs that supported the university's summer bridge program. Several students in the program approached me to disclose the "boot camp"–style psychological hazing they were being forced to endure by the people administering the bridge program . . . . I took a critical race approach to the writing course, and students came to me to ask how they could be reading Michelle Alexander's work on the New Jim Crow in my class but then be subjected to this hazing elsewhere in the same program. These bridge program administrators were people of color themselves, but they had the ear of whites in the university's upper administration. These POCs and the white upper administration felt that I was misreading the situation, and they saw me as the enemy. The head WPA, a tenured white woman—I definitely came to see her as an ally. She trusted me; she believed me. She didn't try to rationalize away my experience and perspective on the problem, and she used her privilege to support me and advocate for me and the bridge students. She gained my confidence through her actions. She not only trusted me, but she also showed me what she would do when she had an opportunity to support me in a committed way.

Allyship is not a choice, it's an everyday practice. So many self-identify as allies because they want the cookie. More important than being an ally, though, is being an accomplice. An accomplice is someone who gives something up, who puts something on the line, who is willing to be critiqued, who is willing to lose something. An ally, on the other hand, just writes an article about racism in order to get points. An ally seeks to understand; an accomplice is willing to do the work.

In response to an earlier draft of this chapter, one reviewer rightfully stated that my essay simply argued that if white WPAs would "open themselves up to others' opinions," African American experience could be centered within WPA scholarship and practice. "It all reads as too easy to achieve," the reviewer stated. That reviewer's assessment was spot-on.

As I returned to the interview transcripts and put the voices of black WPAs and WPAs of color front and center in these sections of my essay, I came to realize more clearly how "opening oneself up to others' opinions" won't happen in a truly meaningful way if one does not first examine, in a substantive way, how white privilege operates in one's own educational and professional experiences. As one black WPA said in the comment above, "An accomplice is someone who gives something up, who puts something on the line, who is willing to be critiqued, who is willing to lose something"— but to make these sacrifices white WPAs also need to do something that we're all too often able to ignore: critically examining and personally acknowledging what privilege we have, how we have gained this privilege, and what it means to put that privilege on the line.

James Baldwin, in his 1963 lecture "The Negro Child—His Self-Image," forces teachers to consider how and why racism operates to create and sustain white supremacy. "Black men were brought here as a source of cheap labor" and "were indispensable to the economy," he explains, so "[i]n order to justify the fact that men were treated as though they were animals, the white republic had to brainwash itself into believing that they were, indeed, animals and *deserved* to be treated like animals." What's especially important to our present collection is how this white supremacy is sustained by US education:

> Therefore it is almost impossible for any Negro child to discover anything about his actual history. The reason is that this "animal," once he suspects his own worth, once he starts believing that he is a man, has begun to attack the entire power structure. This is why America has spent such a long time keeping the Negro in his place. . . . It was a deliberate policy hammered into place in order to make money from black flesh. (290)

This "deliberate policy" to deny humanity to and do physical and psychological violence to black lives underscores the complexity of performing allyship in the way that one black WPA articulated it in the second extended interview excerpt above: "An ally is someone who believes a person of color and doesn't try to rationalize away the person's experiences and perceptions of racism." White WPAs need to acknowledge, more deeply understand, and contribute to efforts to dismantle systematic educational practices that aim to "kee[p] the Negro in his [or her] place."

White WPAs need to be active in these efforts, though, working alongside rather than relying on black WPAs and WPAs of color to do the work of educating everyone else. Such a perspective itself—"Why don't we simply ask black WPAs what they want us to do?"—speaks to the ignorance of both black and white experience that white privilege affords. As Baldwin writes,

> Even today, so brainwashed is this republic that people seriously ask in what they suppose to be good faith, "What does the Negro want?" I've heard a great many asinine questions in my life, but that is perhaps the most asinine and perhaps the most insulting. But the point here is that people who ask that

question, thinking that they ask it in good faith, are really the victims in this conspiracy to make Negroes believe they are less than human.

In order for me to live, I decided very early that some mistake had been made somewhere. I was not a "nigger" even though you called me one. But if I was a "nigger" in your eyes, there was something about *you*—there was something *you* needed. I had to realize when I was very young that I was none of those things I was told I was. . . . I had been invented by white people, and I knew enough about life by this time to understand that whatever you invent, whatever you project, is you! So where we are now is that a whole country of people believe I'm a "nigger," and I *don't*, and the battle's on! Because if I am not what I've been told I am, then it means that *you're* not what *you* thought you were *either!* (290–91)

Reread the WPA narratives of Perryman-Clark and Craig and Carmen Kynard through this lens. Like Baldwin, their resistance to white supremacy that would undermine their "ethos, power, and authority" ("Troubling the Boundaries" 55) is their assertion that "I am not what I've been told I am." If and when white WPAs like me try to rationalize away black WPAs' interpretation of their experience and fail to recognize their acts of self-definition, *we're* not what we thought we were *either!*

In his plenary address at the 2016 CWPA Conference, Asao B. Inoue traces how racist norms within higher education have encouraged white WPAs like me to think about who we are. He begins his talk by forcing his audience of CWPA colleagues to consider the people who are not sitting beside them at the conference plenary session because systematic racism in US education never gave them the chance: the people "who are *not* our students, who for larger historically and structurally racist reasons have yet to be eligible to be our students, and for those who for similar reasons have yet to be eligible to be here with us [at the CWPA conference] or run writing programs or teach writing classes" (134). Moving to the space of the writing classroom itself, Inoue articulates the racist logics that inform normative assumptions about language difference and language standards and suggests that "white teachers [are] not always in the best position to make decisions about our writing classes or our students of color, [and are] not in the best position to judge our students of color or their writing" (137). Finally, he says pointedly to his predominantly white audience in the CWPA, "[Y]ou get to be here because others were systematically denied access. Your success is a product of racism" (138).

White allies operate with self-awareness about this privilege and are motivated to put this unearned privilege on the line when they have an opportunity to support and advocate for a person of color—and they don't "just go away when difficulty appears." This ability to effortlessly "go away" when colleagues experience racism comes, of course, from white privilege. Admittedly, I myself often feel most psychologically comfortable acting with what Inoue describes as "the white dispositions embodied in most hegemonic academic discourses": not making others feel uncomfortable, not calling people out, not being pointed and direct, not being impolite (138). For example, when I'm leading professional development sessions for writing faculty about language diversity, how do I respond when particular faculty argue that "it's all well and good to respect people's home languages, but at the end of the day they all need to write Standard English if they want to get a job"? I always speak back to that perspective, to be sure—"Workplace discrimination against minority employees might seem like it's about language, but that's just because it's a seemingly more acceptable way to discriminate than based on their race or ethnicity"—but too often, Inoue makes me realize, I embody white dispositions in my actions. I always respond to but don't often call out faculty when they make racist statements about language difference; I critique and create mentoring plans for faculty but don't make them uncomfortable when their grading practices clearly penalize students for not conforming to Standard English conventions. In effect, I naturally work to sustain my own psychological comfort and privilege instead of adopting other means to advance social justice for all students and faculty in our writing programs.

Toward the end of his plenary address at CWPA, Inoue poses a series of questions that prompt the crowd of mostly white writing program administrators to reflect on the sources and effects of their privilege. "Is it possible," Inoue asks, "that you have been and are racist because of a white racial *habitus* and a set of whitely ways that you embody, not out of choice or intention but out of necessity and luck of birth?" (152). Yes, I answer. "Is it possible that along with your hard work, this white racial *habitus* and your whitely ways have granted you privileges and benefits at the expense of others?" (152). Absolutely, I say. Writing program administration as a discipline and as a practice has operated in part by doing violence to black bodies and minds, using a range of tools—textbooks, feedback on writing, formal assessments—to define them as "less than" and, in turn, secure privileged positions for whites, who then seem more competent to apply these normalized standards. This way of creating and sustaining white power in writing program administration is not socially just. Dismantling these structures, however, requires more than just good intentions from white WPAs. Instead, it demands a deep-seated commitment from white WPAs to examine how privilege has operated in their educational and professional lives and a willingness to step out of habitually embodied white dispositions and work alongside black WPAs and WPAs of Color for the cause of social justice.

"DELIVER THE TYPE OF ADVICE, SUPPORT, OR FEEDBACK I'M SEEKING": MENTORSHIP AS ALLYSHIP

I think of allyship and mentorship as intersecting at some moments but parallel at other times. Mentors who are also allies—they are someone who, because of their racial and class privilege, might not always share the same experiences navigating the spaces of academia but support me through those experiences. For me, academia is not always intuitive. The intellectual work of critical reading and research was intuitive, but the norms of how people communicate within the academy, how they form partnerships, how they understand how conferences work, how departments work—I had to work hard to understand that. One white ally, a male tenured professor at another university and at the time an Executive Committee member of CWPA—he had never met me before or read my work, but after my presentation to the EC, he supported my statements right away, and he came up to me after the meeting to say that he would help me however and whenever I needed it, and he encouraged me to stay in contact with him throughout my graduate work and into the job market. That directness was helpful to me. It's very hard for someone in liminal spaces to go to someone and ask them to be your mentor, to ask them a question about how to apply for a specific job, to know how to do a job talk, to understand how to request letters of recommendation. These things can be a bit confusing, especially for first-generation scholars of color, and this ally's directness was very helpful. Mentoring someone who is from a marginalized group, being very direct and saying "I want to help you" is very helpful, but doing it not in a patronizing way and instead just leaving things open to the scholar of color to determine whatever type of relationship she needs to or would like to have. The communication is very specific, allows me to determine what I'd like to ask of them, what's my goal. I'm the one determining the nature of the mentoring relationship—and the ally always follows through and delivers the type of advice, support, or feedback I'm seeking.

All but one of the faculty in our rhetoric and composition graduate program are white, but we have committed to actively recruiting, educating, and mentoring students of color into our graduate programs. We make it an explicit goal in our grad recruitment to admit students from racial minority groups, marginalized gender and sexual identity groups, and first-generation college students. This work doesn't stop with simply admitting more students into graduate programs, either. And we don't only look for graduate students who are the perfect "fit" for the research that we all do. We openly talk about and affirm our commitment to providing the types of mentoring, teaching, and research support necessary for a diverse group of graduate students to pursue the research projects they propose. We talk about the types of courses we would need to offer to best support a particular cohort of students and the types of guidance they might need throughout all stages of the doctoral program and into the academic job search. And as we've continued to have these conversations and do this teaching and mentoring year after year, we now see that diversity not only is an ethical goal but also enhances the intellectual activity of our program. Increasing diversity in the program brings different experiences and worldviews into the discipline. Our work as faculty and as mentors is to help graduate students learn how to use these experiences and worldviews as frames through which to carry out their research and teaching.

In July 2018, the writing programs at my school—the Academic Writing Program, the Professional Writing Program, and the Writing Center—invited a black WPA to campus in order to guide us through the initial stages of drafting a diversity plan to guide our writing programs. Part of our discussion focused on graduate-student recruitment. One key piece of addressing racism in our writing programs, this scholar explained, is to begin recruiting at undergraduate programs at HBCUs, of which there are several within our region, rather than only recruiting MA-level minority students who've already sought out our program. What the two extended comments above—one from a WPA of color and the other from a white WPA—reinforce, however, is the fact that building and sustaining a racially and ethnically diverse graduate program requires more than that active recruitment. It also requires doing the important mentoring and teaching work within the program that supports those students and helps them to develop into scholars who can use their experience as valued resources for their scholarly investigations. As the first passage in particular suggests, white allies think about this mentoring not in terms of addressing intellectual deficits but rather helping students from historically underrepresented groups understand and act on what white privilege afforded them in terms of knowledge and experiences about academic norms. White allies, too, help black graduate students to develop both research projects and a teacherly ethos that builds on and speaks to their social experiences and language use. As the white WPA's comment suggests, some of this planning for mentoring and teaching should happen during discussions of graduate applications, and white allies frame these conversations not in terms of burdensome extra work but rather as critical efforts for dismantling structural racism in the academy and building more socially just writing programs and more socially just disciplines of composition studies and of writing program administration.

Indeed, even as white WPAs and writing studies faculty carry out this active recruitment and mentoring to support black graduate students and other graduate students of color, they must carry out this work, as the WPA of color argues above, "not in a patronizing way." Rather, they must create communication channels that allow the student to "determin[e] the nature of the mentoring relationship," and they must "always follow through and deliver the type of advice, support, or feedback" the graduate student is seeking. This work, of course, requires white faculty to critically examine their emotional dispositions toward and their perceptions of their cultural competencies to mentor black students. While she's writing about the secondary education context in particular, eighth-grade teacher Chrysanthius Lathan provides a relevant description of typical white attitudes and assumptions about mentoring black students:

> Based on conversations with colleagues and my observations, I think that many whites live in fear of their good faith actions being labeled as racist. Rather than facing that fear and seeing what they can learn about themselves from the process, many white teachers seem to believe that a better alternative would be to pair students with teachers who look and sound like them, or like people in their families, in the name of having a positive role model or mentor. There's no doubt that we need more teachers of color in our schools, but we also have to deal with the situation that exists today. Many white

teachers are discouraged, believing that they are ill-equipped to meet the needs of students of color simply because they don't have the same experiences as them. In response, they freeze. (303)

Lathan demands that white teachers acknowledge but then work through these fears: "Just because you are a white teacher and do not experience life through the same lens as your students of color doesn't mean you can't build an environment where realness, rigor, and relationships abound in your classroom" (305).

A critical part of building these relationships is being open to criticism and critique when graduate students of color provide it. This type of response—being open, not defensive—is difficult for many white faculty like me because direct criticism disrupts those "white dispositions" Inoue exposes. For example, during my first seven years as WPA at the University of Maryland, my colleagues and I have worked to integrate readings and discussions related to race and linguistic diversity into the curriculum for our Approaches to College Composition graduate course, which prepares graduate students for their first semester of teaching first-year writing. This curriculum does not simply shoehorn race and linguistic diversity issues into one or two weeks at the end of the semester but rather integrates these issues through the entirety of the syllabus. For example, we read Adam Banks's analysis of digital griots during our week on process and postprocess theories, we read Geneva Smither-man's work on the connection between African American cultural worldviews and rhetorical forms during weeks on teaching the canons of invention and arrangement, and we read essays by Cheryl Johnson and Arnetha Ball and Ted Lardner in a week about teacher ethos and efficacy.

While my colleagues and I had long believed it was important to integrate discussion of race, ethnicity, and linguistic diversity into our graduate course preparing new teachers of writing, these topics became even more urgent as several acts of racial violence occurred on campus in the past two years. In May 2016, University of Maryland police pepper-sprayed black students at an off-campus gradua-tion party (Zirin). One year later, in April 2017, students in a Terps for Trump group chalked anti-Dreamer messages such as "Deport the Dreamers" all over campus. A short time later, in May 2017, a noose was found in the kitchen of the Phi Kappa Theta fraternity house (Wells). And then in that same month, Second Lieutenant Richard Collins III, an African American student from nearby Bowie State, a HBCU, was stabbed and killed by Sean Urbanski, a white University of Maryland student who was a member of a racist Facebook group, Alt-Reich: Nation (Zirin). Black students shared their anger, frustrations, and fears using the hashtag #FearThe Turtle on Twitter ("UMD Students"). With students' experiences with on-campus racism in mind, during the fall 2017 semester we added a week explicitly focused on racism, drawing on the various "Teaching after Charlottesville" resources that emerged in the wake of white supremacist rallies in Virginia in August 2017.

During the first month of the spring 2018 semester, however, four graduate students wrote to the department chair expressing their concern that they didn't feel adequately prepared to handle sensitive issues around race and diversity and that they didn't feel as though they knew exactly how the WPAs would respond if students filed complaints about them related to how they handled race and diversity issues in class. My initial response in this situation, in a meeting with the chair, associate chair, and fellow WPA (the acting director of academic writing, as the director was on sabbatical that semester), was to try to rationalize away the concerns, explaining that there must be some misunderstanding because of all the topics we had integrated into the graduate course preparing them for their teaching. After I had aired those arguments to rationalize away the students' concerns about their preparation concerning race and writing pedagogy, however, I called to mind the insight from the black WPA I interviewed who argued that we should define white WPA allies not simply by the programs they institute and the values they express about racism and ethnolinguistic diversity but also by "the kinds of responses they have when faced with problems concerning diversity." While the programmatic goals related to diversity that WPAs pursue obviously are important, actions define white allies.

With this perspective in mind, the writing programs have responded to these calls for more support, guidance, and preparation in more comprehensive, substantive ways. For example, we are bringing a WPA of color to campus to lead a professional development session on antiracist composition pedagogy; we invited a black WPA to campus to consult with the writing programs as we draft a diversity plan that will articulate our programs' mission and vision in terms of antiracism, diversity, and inclusion and outline plans for bring this vision to life through our hiring, curriculum, assessment, management, and professional development activities; and we continue to add readings, activities, and writing projects exploring race and diversity in our Approaches to College Composition graduate course.

Even so, as the WPA of color I quoted earlier said, simply looking at the programs one develops and the stances toward racism one develops do not alone define one as an ally. Rather, an ally is someone who responds to support black students and colleagues and who actively pursues antiracism in times of challenge. My white privilege operated in my immediate response to criticism, as I tried to rationalize away people's experiences with explanations and defenses of our curriculum and pedagogy. The black WPAs and WPAs of color I interviewed, however, prompted me to reflect on what the aims of such a curriculum for GTA training is and to acknowledge that if and when the GTAs express concerns, my first response must be to listen to their experiences and their concerns. Indeed, as Krista Ratcliffe contends in *Rhetorical Listening*, we need to train our "ears [to] hear criticism . . . as an invitation to dialogue [rather than] as blame" (91).

Listening deeply to these experiences and being attuned to this personal white discomfort can and must be a source of sustaining motivation to create better living and learning conditions for our black graduate students and black colleagues. As activist Paul Kivel warns, however, white allies "should remind ourselves that, although we want to be trusted, trust is not the issue" (210). "We are not fighting racism," he argues, "so that people of color will *trust* us" (210). Rather, trust builds over time based on how white academics treat black colleagues and black graduate students—not expecting them to conform to the "white racial *habitus*" of academia (Inoue 150) but instead supporting their "rhetorical abilities as WPAs of color to use [their] own voices as agents of change, to define and speak for ourselves" (Craig and Perryman-Clark, "Troubling the Boundaries" 55).

"WHITE FACULTY NEED TO BE ABLE TO SAY, 'THIS IS HURTING OUR STUDENTS'": COMPOSING SOCIAL JUSTICE MISSIONS FOR WRITING PROGRAMS

I often find diversity initiatives to be very surface-level and aesthetic. Administrators say, "We're going to hire a specific group of people," but when it has to do with the inner workings of a department or a writing program, the decisions are still made by the white, Eurocentric people. Allyship instead involves not just creating the space for people to exist within the department, but also saying, "We want your voice in the decision-making process as well." Any policy that affects people of color, if it's created without directly consulting people of color, it's a useless policy. We're really good at hiring diverse faculty, but not great at keeping them. We're not great at creating space where people of color feel like they're making an impact in the department. If you're a colleague or a friend to someone, when you're having a faculty member who's dealing with a situation that feels toxic, examine how much decision-making power the people of color have within that space. Just because the space looks diverse doesn't mean that it fully supports diversity.

Textbook companies have brought in outside writing studies experts from R1 institutions to talk with HBCUs, but these kinds of things need to be reciprocated. Moreover, our true alliances are with our students. We always are trying to negotiate that divide between what the experts are saying is best for us and what we know locally is best for our students. As WPA at a HBCU, I am always encouraging my faculty to do what works best for their students—as long as they can substantiate that it works. How do we get faculty at HBCUs to lead the conversation nationally, as opposed to always only relying on the faculty from prestigious R1 institutions? Building bonds, connections with faculty in other HBCUs—that's been important, because too often outside people think they know what is best for us. We can build alliances among our own faculty at HBCUs, create strength interinstitutionally across HBCUs, and then build out from there to begin being heard in these larger conversations in writing studies. . . . We need to think about multiple models of creating antiracist administrative and pedagogical practice: one is the top-down model of R1 institutions telling institutions like HBCUs what to do, and the other is the bottom-up model of HBCUs describing and theorizing what works best for black students at their institutions and then telling R1 institutions what to do.

People of color feel they are overburdened with race initiatives, that whenever a problem with racism comes up they have to be the spokesperson to deal with it. The irony is that the more they talked openly, the more they felt like the environment they were in was toxic. They were relied on to figure out issues of race, but they were not listened to—any time they spoke, they were silenced in some way. Conversely, too often white faculty . . . don't know about diversity initiatives on campus or sometimes don't even know about diversity initiatives in the writing program. Those white faculty say they want to be educated about things, for example, like Asao Inoue's antiracist assessment practices, but people of color often feel like when they do this education, they are not being listened to when they actually describe the problems on campus or in the writing program. . . . The more that white folks can speak in precise ways about the race-based initiatives on their campus—hiring, assessment, pedagogy—the more comfortable they are in talking about race, in creating environments where POC could speak. It's important for white faculty to talk about race-based initiatives, to be more articulate about how they talk about race. White faculty need to be able to say, "This is hurting our students."

During my first seven years as WPA of our professional writing program, which delivers the upper-division general education writing course at our university, I tried to make language diversity an area of focus in our professional development and our pedagogy. I led full-day professional development sessions on topics such as helping students build on nonstandardized varieties of English and working with multilingual writers, and on three other occasions we hosted nationally recognized composition scholars to facilitate professional development sessions on linguistic diversity in composition classrooms. I've written regularly about the issue for our program's monthly newsletter, and our writing program's reading group discussed my archive-based research about a group of faculty who responded to the CCCC's "Students' Right to Their Own Language" policy by designing a curriculum for black and Puerto Rican first-year composition students. One critical piece missing from these activities, however, is integrating these values toward language diversity into mission and vision statements that articulate a social justice mission for our program's teaching and research.

My failure to initiate the process for composing these statements has had significant consequences. The lack of a focused mission statement informing our professional development activities about language diversity allow some professional writing faculty to fall back on and feel secure in their instincts to demand Standard English only because students "need" it to get a job. In their comments during professional development sessions and during individual mentoring meetings, these faculty echo Richard Rodriguez, perceiving me to be too "sentimental" toward students' voices and identities and instead identifying with those "unsentimental" teachers who steadfastly carry out their mission to help the "disadvantaged child" (Villanueva 17). Victor Villanueva interrogated this pedagogical stance in a 1987 *English Journal* article, arguing that this romanticized vision of teachers working with historically underrepresented groups allows them to feel comfortable in their decisions to ban non–Standard English dialects in the classroom.

Villanueva believed that this vision of teachers helping "the disadvantaged child" appeals to many teachers because in it the "complexities of the minority are rendered simply—not easy—but easily understood" (19). Villanueva's insights underscore the fact that as a WPA I need to do more than simply provide teachers with a list of classroom activities that would promote language diversity and work toward antiracist ends. We need to compose mission and vision statements that focus our collective sights on these goals. These statements in turn can inform moments in professional development, building on Arnetha Ball and Ted Lardner's work, for teachers to identify and probe the sources of their knowledge of and attitudes toward nonstandardized languages and toward students of color. This self-examination would be a critical step toward helping teachers reimagine their classrooms as spaces in which students develop a range of rhetorical skills and cultural competencies they could use to negotiate the varying and sometimes conflicting cultural demands from families, communities, schools, and workplaces.

Moreover, what I hear in the two interview excerpts from black WPAs at the start of this section is the imperative to articulate more precisely—for our faculty, for myself as WPA, and ultimately for our students—ways that our mission and vision for the writing program align with and build on campus initiatives for diversity and inclusion. These mission and vision statements become the foundation for curricular design and pedagogical training that enables faculty to bring this mission and this vision to life in their classes. At the same time, this work demands that I, as a white WPA leading a large, overwhelmingly white faculty contingent, acknowledge how white privilege and white institutional racism makes this work difficult, in that I must wholeheartedly sacrifice my privilege of steering clear of discomfort when faculty challenge this vision and say that we must teach Standard English only.

Christine Tardy outlines the challenges of both drafting these types of programmatic statements concerning language diversity and racism and implementing them in administrators' and teachers' daily practices, yet crafting them nevertheless is an important task for WPAs to undertake. The invention and drafting process can prompt important reflection on how the writing programs are related to the broader goals of the institution's mission and general education programs. At my school, for example, the academic writing and professional writing courses are Fundamental Studies requirements that all students must take, but while we WPAs meet regularly with the other Fundamental Studies program directors (Oral Communication and Mathematics), we have not explored or articulated specific ways that our courses prepare students for or build on other General Education requirements, particularly the courses that fulfill the "Understanding Plural Societies" and "Cultural Competence" distribution requirements.

The black WPA whose interview is excerpted above prompts us to look to WPAs at HBCUs for theories, pedagogy, and curricula that models effective practice in culturally responsible writing courses. Both David Green and Alexandria Lockett's contributions to this volume provide important heuristics for thinking through the challenges of connecting core writing courses to other general education courses that advance antiracism and social justice, and the writing program at another HBCU, Winston-Salem State University, having just earned the 2018 CCCC Writing Program Certificate of Excellence, provides another model of how to synthesize writing course goals with the institution's vision of "develop[ing] leaders who advance social justice by serving the world with compassion and commitment" ("Strategic Plan").

At my institution, where just over 50 percent of the student body is nonwhite, the social, political, and pedagogical value in looking to and learning from HBCUs can be more readily seen—although it will, again, necessarily require critically interrogating the racist assumptions about language and bodily difference that uphold many teachers' devotion to teaching Standard English only. Once in place, these mission and vision statements, as Staci Perryman-Clark's work at Western Michigan University demonstrates, guide both long-term planning and short-term decision making, from assignment design, textbook development, assessment, and retention initiatives to hiring, professional development, teacher evaluation, student support, and even new-course development. For these reasons, drafting this mission and vision statement will be the foremost concern in our writing programs' activities this coming semester, which will in turn inform the programs' diversity plan that we craft and then implement in the subsequent semesters.

What, though, about white WPAs at predominantly white institutions? And how willing are all of us, as white WPAs, to do this "uncomfortable" (from the perspective of dominant white emotional dispositions) work of challenging ourselves and our white teaching faculty to recognize our racial privilege, to critique the institutions through which we have been elevated because of this privilege, and to listen to and learn from WPAs and faculty at HBCUs toward the ends of collectively creating antiracist pedagogies that benefit black students, other students of color, and white students alike?

CONCLUSION: "DON'T JUST GO AWAY WHEN DIFFICULTY APPEARS."

We theorized and imagined effective strategies for building allyship and thought through how racial allies might equally share in the stakes of those who represent the historically disenfranchised. We candidly spoke about what this said about white privilege. We collectively reflected on how white faculty must consider how much of their own privilege they are willing to forfeit for the cause of social justice.

—Collin Craig and Staci Perryman-Clark,
"Troubling the Boundaries Revisited"

The lack of sustained treatment on issues of whiteness and racism in the [*Writing Program Administration*] journal isn't surprising. The way I've seen most compositionists deal with racism and their own whiteness is to have good intentions and then avoid the topic altogether because that's not what they do, or they're not experts, or others do that work.

—Asao B. Inoue, "Racism in Writing
Programs and the CWPA"

My earliest drafts of this conclusion struck resoundingly positive notes:

> To "share in the stakes of those who represent the historically disenfranchised," white WPAs must invest the effort required to create conditions that allow black WPAs to participate in knowledge making at the disciplinary and institutional levels; in turn, they will share in the rewards that come from an invigorated and reimagined scholarly discipline that features new voices, new narratives, and new theories about how we write, teach writing, and run writing programs.

Since writing passages like that one, I've returned countless times to the transcripts of my interviews with black WPAs and WPAs of color; I've read through the entire manuscript of this collection; I've read the growing body of scholarship on race and writing program administration; and I've used all of that material to reflect on and make new meaning about my own experiences as a white, male WPA, particularly during the current moments of racial violence against black people and other people of color on my campus.

I'm realizing that I struck those resoundingly positive notes in my earlier conclusion because I find them comforting, because on the outside I want to feel like or project that I'm doing enough when deep down I understand that antiracist work requires sustained, fully committed action and reflection. Inoue, in his plenary address, demanded that we acknowledge how white WPAs' good intentions for antiracist work too often fail to translate into any— let alone any meaningful, transformative—practice. And Carmen Kynard, in her essay in this collection, argues: "Without a radical break from the very ideological origins of black subjugation, such easily made solutions will, at best, only cater to the interests of white comfort and white fragility" (29).

It is important to end the essay on these less optimistic notes, then, to underscore what's at stake for white WPAs in contributing to antiracist work within the field of writing program administration and within our local writing programs. The emerging body of scholarship on race and WPA work helps us to begin developing strategies for curricular redesign, textbook selection, assessment, professional development and the training of new faculty, and support of undergraduate and graduate students of color (Burrows; S. Craig; Sanchez and Branson; Zenger). At the same time, these practices need to be carried out with an awareness of and motivation to disrupt the reality that "[black] bodies are visibly marked in institutional spaces . . . [and] in disciplinary spaces" and are then defined and described in the terms of racist white logics in order to maintain the status quo (Craig and Perryman-Clark, "Troubling the Boundaries" 54). As Baldwin forces us to acknowledge, the systematic racism and microaggressions that reinforce particular white understandings of black bodies, black intellect, and black language do not ultimately say as much about black people as they say about white people and their need to maintain this social order.

The CWPA has made some important steps to begin examining disciplinary and organizational racism with its recent publications and conferences, such as the featured speaker at the 2018 conference from Black Lives Matter Sacramento, Sonia Lewis, who delivered, in her words, an "unapologetically uncomfortable" talk titled "Unpacking the Lingering and Destructive Ideologies of Colonialism, Slavery, and Capitalism." The WPA-GO Think Tank on Social Justice in Organizational and Disciplinary Spaces has done even more sustained work on these issues, having held roundtables that consistently focus on the topics of race and social justice at several consecutive CCCC and CWPA conferences.

As one WPA of color I interviewed explained, however, "It's hard work, and we can't take a single day off. It's constant work—day after day after day." WPAs can sometimes find comfort in feeling that they're doing important work in "putting out fires" that flare up during the semester—a group of students bring complaints about a teacher, a teacher falls ill or resigns at spring break—or in dealing with everyday programmatic issues such as scheduling, budgeting, and teacher evaluation. White WPAs must begin to see these day-to-day concerns with scheduling, budgeting, teacher evaluation, and so on through the frame of race, power, and privilege: Who's teaching which courses and why, and who's not teaching—and who's never even had the chance to earn teaching positions—and why? What standards do we use to evaluate teacher effectiveness, and how do dispositions toward race and language diversity and teaching practices involving that diversity factor into these evaluations? Equally important, white WPAs need to make time for and engage in the sustained, long-term, challenging work of developing a mission and vision of antiracist and social justice for their writing programs. The narratives from Collin Craig, Staci Perryman-Clark, Carmen Kynard, Asao B. Inoue, and the many black WPAs and WPAs of color whom I've interviewed have made clear the difficulties they face within their local institutions and within the wider discipline. White WPA allies must not "just go away when [this] difficulty appears."

WORKS CITED

Baldwin, James. "A Talk to Teachers [The Negro Child—His Self-Image]." Watson, Hagopian, and Au, pp. 287–93.

Ball, Arnetha, and Ted Lardner. "Dispositions toward Language: Teacher Constructs of Knowledge and the Ann Arbor Black English Case." *College Composition and Communication*, vol. 48, no.4, Dec. 1997, pp. 469–85.

Banks, Adam J. *Digital Griots: African American Rhetoric in a Multimedia Age*. National Council of Teachers of English, 2011.

Burrows, Cedric D. "The Yardstick of Whiteness in Composition Textbooks." *WPA: Writing Program Administration*, vol., 39, no. 2, Spring 2016, pp. 42–46.

Craig, Collin Lamont, and Staci M. Perryman-Clark. "Troubling the Boundaries: (De) Constructing WPA Identities at the Intersections of Race and Gender." *WPA: Writing Program Administration*, vol. 34, no. 2, Spring 2011, pp. 37–58.

———. "Troubling the Boundaries Revisited: Moving towards Change as Things Stay the Same." *WPA: Writing Program Administration*, vol. 39, no. 2, Spring 2016, pp. 20–26.

Craig, Sherri. "A Story-less Generation: Emergent WPAs of Color and the Loss of Identity through Absent Narratives." *WPA: Writing Program Administration*, vol. 39, no. 2, Spring 2016, pp. 16–20.

García de Müeller, Genevieve, and Iris Ruiz. "Race, Silence, and Writing Program Administration: A Qualitative Study of U.S. College Writing Programs." *WPA: Writing Program Administration,* vol. 40, no. 2, June 2017, pp. 19–39.

Inoue, Asao B. "Racism in Writing Programs and the CWPA." *WPA: Writing Program Administration,* vol. 40, no.1, Fall 2016, pp.134–54.

Johnson, Cheryl. "Disinfecting Dialogues." *Pedagogy: The Question of Impersonation,* edited by Jane Gallop, Indiana UP, 1995, pp. 129–37.

Kivel, Paul. "How White People Can Serve as Allies to People of Color in the Struggle to End Racism." *White Privilege: Essential Readings on the Other Side of Racism.* Ed. Paula S. Rothenberg. 5th ed. Macmillan, 2016, pp. 207–13.

Lathan, Chrysanthius. "Dear White Teacher." Watson, Hagopian, and Au, pp. 299–305.

Ratcliffe, Krista. *Rhetorical Listening: Identification, Gender, Whiteness.* Southern Illinois UP, 2005.

Royster, Jacqueline Jones. "When the First Voice You Hear Is Not Your Own." *College Composition and Communication,* vol. 47, no. 1, Feb. 1996, pp. 29–40.

Sanchez, James Chase, and Tyler S. Branson. "The Role of Composition Programs in De-Normalizing Whiteness in the University: Programmatic Approaches to Anti-Racist Pedagogies." *WPA: Writing Program Administration,* vol. 39, no. 2, Spring 2016, pp. 47–52.

Smitherman, Geneva. *Talkin and Testifyin: The Language of Black America.* 1977. Wayne State UP, 1986.

"Strategic Plan 2016–2021: Vision and Mission." Winston-Salem State University, 2016, www.wssu.edu/strategic-plan/temp. aspx?name=vision-mission.

Tardy, Christine M. "Enacting and Transforming Local Language Policies." *College Composition and Communication,* vol. 62, no. 4, June 2011, pp. 634–61.

"UMD Students Chronicle Racist Campus Experiences with '#FearTheTurtle.'" *Joe Clair Morning Show.* WPGC, Washington,

DC, 22 May 2017, wpgc.radio.com/blogs/joe-clair-morning-show/umd-students-chronicle-racist-campus-experiences-'#fear theturtle'.

Villanueva, Victor, Jr. "Whose Voice Is It Anyway? Rodriguez' Speech in Retrospect." *English Journal,* vol. 76, no. 8, Dec. 1987, pp. 17–21.

Watson, Dyan, Jesse Hagopian, and Wayne Au, eds. *Teaching for Black Lives.* Rethinking Schools, 2018.

Wells, Carrie. "Noose Found in University of Maryland College Park Frat House." *Baltimore Sun,* 4 May 2017, www.baltimore sun.com/news/maryland/education/higher-ed/bs-md-umd-noose-20170503-story.html.

Wible, Scott. "Pedagogies of the 'Students' Right' Era: The Language Curriculum Research Group's Project for Linguistic Diversity." *College Composition and Communication,* vol. 57, no. 3, Feb. 2006, pp. 442–78.

WPA-GO Think Tank on Social Justice in Organizational and Disciplinary Spaces. "Think Tank for Racial and Social Justice in the Writing Program Administrators–Graduate Organization and Beyond." Conference on College Composition and Communication, 17 Mar. 2017, Oregon Convention Center, Portland, OR. Interactive think tank.

Zenger, Amy A. "Notes on Race in Transnational Writing Program Administration." *WPA: Writing Program Administration,* vol. 39, no. 2, Spring 2016, pp. 26–31.

Zirin, Dave. "A Lynching on the University of Maryland Campus." *Nation* 22 May 2017, www.thenation.com/article/lynching-uni versity-maryland-campus/.

5

Black Student Success Models: Institutional Profiles of Writing Programs

Staci M. Perryman-Clark and Collin Lamont Craig

IN THE PREVIOUS CHAPTERS OF THIS COLLECTION, contributors have addressed the political and theoretical implications associated with black perspectives in WPA work. Much of this discussion has focused on how WPA scholars and practitioners might foster stronger alliance building across institutional contexts and identity politics. While this work addresses the sociopolitical implications for engaging Afrocentric theory and inclusion in WPA work and scholarship, we now wish to conclude the discussion in a way that moves from the political and theoretical to the pragmatic. Thus, in this space, we wish to address the pedagogical imperative: more precisely, we provide a framework for success with black perspectives in writing program administration and briefly highlight and showcase a few writing programs that actively engage Afrocentric theories and black perspectives in the intellectual work that teachers and scholars do in their writing programs. We use our overview of writing programmatic models and profiles as an introduction to the Web-based space that includes resources from contributions to our collection.

These profiles include Western Michigan University's first-year writing-intensive program (ENGL 1050I), Spelman University's writing program, and Huston-Tillotson University's first-year writing program. We have carefully chosen one ally-based model and two HBCU models. We provide one example of an ally model to provide a practical example that speaks to the intellectual work outlined by Scott Wible in Chapter 4. We provide two additional examples from HBCU writing programs because we firmly believe that engaging black perspectives in WPA work requires greater inclusion of and focus on HBCU experiences. It is our sincerest hope that rhetoric and composition might begin to look to HBCUs for direction on the best practices that emphasize Afrocentric theory and pedagogy.

RETHINKING WPA RESOURCE SPACES: INCLUDING BLACK PERSPECTIVES

One of the largest sources for WPAs who require examples of writing program profiles for professional development is the Council of Writing Program Administrators' website, http://wpacouncil. org. Two of the largest sets of resources on this site include the Assessment Gallery and the list of writing program websites by state. When scanning these materials, one will notice that not a single HBCU writing program or profile is included in the Assessment Gallery, nor are any HBCU writing program websites listed. Moreover, the only evidence of any potential connections to cultural competences includes a report from a 2008 WPA Task Force on Internationalization, which has not been updated or revised since its final draft was published on the CWPA' website. One of the recommendations from this taskforce asks that the WPA website include more materials and resources on international programs, specifically noting the following recommendations:

> More links could be made to existing international sites, such as CompFAQ's international page and other organizations of writing researchers, teachers, and administrators (the European Association of Research on Learning and Instruction's Writing SIG; the International Association for the Improvement of Mother Tongue Education; the Australian Association of Writing Programs; the Simpósio Internacional de Estudos de Gêneros Textuais [International Symposium on Genre Studies]; the European Association for the Teaching of Academic Writing; the European Writing Centers Association; the Association for Writing Development in Higher

Education; InterLAE; the International Conference for the Study of Speech, Writing, and Context; the Canadian Association of Teachers of Technical Writing; the newly formed Middle East and North African Writing Centers Association; and so on). (4)

What is interesting about the above recommendations for suggested links to resources is the fact that the only mention of the African diaspora among these international programs is Northern Africa; notice, however, that sub-Saharan Africa is *not* included or offered as a location for stronger global engagement of writing programs.

Speaking specifically of the Assessment Gallery, the gallery aims to provide examples of model assessments and communication strategies. It proposes to provide models "from a range of institutions, from 2-year colleges to R1 universities, that enact the strategies in the NCTE-WPA White Paper [on Writing Assessment in Colleges and Universities]" (par. 4). The NCTE-WPA White Paper outlines the following articulations and understandings of best practices associated with writing assessment:

- The connections among language, literacy, and writing assessment
- The principles of effective writing assessment
- The appropriate, fair, and valid use of writing assessment
- The role and importance of reliability in writing assessment.

We feel great concern about the exclusion of HBCUs and any references to cultural competence, including—and especially—that of African American student writers for several reasons. First, the contributors make the claim that the gallery includes a wide range of institutions, and while this is true in terms of Carnegie institutional classifications, the claim is less accurate with regard to the cultural identities and missions of the various postsecondary institutions. A range that does not include profiles of HBCUs, tribal colleges, or Hispanic-serving institutions, for example, does not reflect the greatest diversity across institutional contexts or models. Second, excluding HBCUs, for example, may potentially suggests that there aren't models at these institutions that align with the best practices identified by the NCTE-WPA White Paper, thereby ignoring the training and intellectual work of rhetoric and composition scholars who teach at these institutions. Third, the mere omission of any references to cultural competence ignores a significant population of students of color enrolled across a wide variety of postsecondary institutions. If the intellectual work presented in this space excludes perspectives of students of color, and, for our purposes, specifically African American students, might this potentially undermine the principle of "appropriate, fair, and valid use of writing assessment"? Fourth, and finally, we see the exclusion of students of color as a missed opportunity to speak to the first principle that connections among language, literacy, and writing assessment be made and emphasized across the wide range of Assessment Gallery profiles. There certainly isn't a shortage of scholarship about the culturally diverse linguistic identities that students bring with them into the composition classroom, and how these identities, more precisely, enhance and contribute to student success in writing assessment (Perryman-Clark, *Afrocentric;* Perryman-Clark, "Who We Are(n't) Assessing"). Why not provide examples of student success in relation to students of culturally diverse linguistic backgrounds?

REVISING THE FRAMEWORK FOR SUCCESS IN POSTSECONDARY WRITING: NEW MODELS FOR SUCCESS WITH BLACK PERSPECTIVES

In the previous section of this chapter, we critiqued the omission of HBCUs and black perspectives from the Assessment Gallery and writing programs listed on the CWPA website. We now would like to direct readers' attention to another significant component from CWPA's website, the Framework for Success in Postsecondary Writing, collaboratively published with NCTE and the National Writing Project. Perhaps, politically and theoretically, the Framework for Success in Postsecondary Writing has become the "go-to" source for WPAs who wish to do advocacy work within governmental, legislative, and institutional contexts. It provides rhetorical arguments for WPAs wishing to articulate and communicate the work that we do in composition to audiences unfamiliar with our intellectual work and discipline. The framework seeks to more accurately define "college-readiness" and "describes the rhetorical and twenty-first-century skills as well as habits of mind and experiences that are critical for college success" ("Executive Summary"). The principles specifically focus on rhetorical knowledge and versatility, critical thinking, writing processes, knowledge of conventions, and composing in a variety of environments.

With reference to the framework, we see an additional missed opportunity to refer to intersectionality as it pertains to racial, cultural, and linguistic diversity and how this framework supports students of these backgrounds. The most recent version of the Framework for Success in Postsecondary Writing omits any mention of cultural and linguistic diversity, although a previous version called for writing educators to be flexible in the assessment of students' written conventional practices, "recogniz[ing] that conventions (such as formal and informal rules of content, organization, style, evidence, citation, mechanics, usage, register, and dialect) are dependent on discipline and context." Yet still neither version of the framework provides a direct recognition of students of racially and linguistically diverse backgrounds in a way that explicitly affirms and celebrates "register[s]" and "dialect[s]" that students bring with them into the classroom.

The case could be made that this framework promotes culturally linguistic principles because one of its recommendations suggests that teachers "help writers develop rhetorical knowledge by providing opportunities and guidance for students to . . . write and analyze a variety of text types to identify . . . the key choices of content, organization, evidence, and language use made by their authors" (10). The problem with such a recommendation is that it is not clear what role "language choice" plays and whether or not all language choices made by both authors and writers are created equally. Further, language choice seems to be the only mention of the use of language by students at all in the entire document. More focused attention to students' language uses and the decisions that govern such uses is needed, and perhaps this may have been the one opportunity to refer to students of color at all; instead, the framework treats students as a homogenous group.

While the Framework on Postsecondary Writing makes limited mention of the uses of language by composition students, the Council of Writing Program Administrators does more directly speak to language in its final report on internationalization, as discussed previously in this chapter. In this report, the CWPA Taskforce on Internationalization uses language issues as one example of an obstacle to the collaboration of WPAs across global contexts. They assert: "For example, language issues may be a major impediment to internationalizing the WPA, but without knowing the linguistic situation at a specific institution, it is impossible to seek ways to draw in writing scholars and teachers." There is no mention of the direct effect that this vague "linguistic situation" has on students. Moreover, language is positioned as an obstacle/liability and not an asset that can help foster collaborations on linguistic diversity across cultural and verbal contexts. The moral of the story is to figure out the linguistic situation on your own. We therefore seek to revise the framework more directly with African American students in mind.

FRAMEWORK FOR SUCCESS: CHARACTERISTICS OF SUCCESSFUL MODELS

In this section, we provide our own framework that identifies what successful institutional programs look like. Once we've identified this framework, we will draw on examples of the institutional models we include in both Chapter 6 and within the webspace extension to this book. But first, we would like to highlight some critical principles for successful writing programs that engage black perspectives in WPA work. Of course, this list is not intended be exhaustive or prescriptive; however, it does provide WPAs with a starting place for critically engaging black students. Furthermore, while some programs may enact one or more of these principles, we wish to showcase those that provide stellar examples reflective of each principle.

Principle 1: Afrocentric pedagogical materials are placed at the center of the curriculum.

In "The Afrocentric Idea in Education," Molefi Kete Asante defines Afrocentric education as the following: "Afrocentricity is a frame of reference wherein phenomena are viewed from the perspective of the African person. The Afrocentric approach seeks in every situation the appropriate centrality of the African person (Asante, 1987). In education, this means that teachers provide students the opportunity to study the world and its people, concepts, and history from an African worldview" (171). Our goal with each of the contributions in our collection is to frame the work that we do as WPAs in our writing programs from the perspective of black diasporic people. Furthermore, we seek to position black perspectives as the central focus of WPA work, and not simply as a peripheral inclusion or extension of a mainstream composition curriculum. For the programs we highlight in Chapter 6 as well as in our extended webspace we see HBCUs as unique opportunities for composition to examine the ways in which their missions and curricula foci center directly on black perspectives, and how this centrality lays a critical foundation for intellectual thought and literacy in higher education. Two examples in our webspace that engage black perspectives with regard to centrality are Alexandria L. Lockett's profile of the Spelman College program and Shawanda Stewart and Brian Stone's profile of the Huston-Tillotson University program. Both profiles underscore the unique roles that HBCUs play in designing Afrocentric pedagogical materials.

With regard to Spelman College, students who enroll in their first-year composition courses, English 103 and 193, are also required to take a course titled African Diaspora and the World (ADW), thereby ensuring that students engage Afrocentricity from a wide range of academic disciplines. While it is common for first-year writing programs across US higher education to coordinate "big questions" or theme-based topics with other disciplines, courses, and programs, exploring Afrocentricity provides a unique opportunity to ensure that perspectives of black people maintain a focus of intellectual knowledge, even as content in skills courses like reading and first-year writing.

Huston-Tillotson's first-year writing program more specifically engages African-centered materials to help students understand the roles of language in their own literate lives. Stewart and Stone specifically designed materials to respond to David F. Green Jr.'s call for "compositionists at HBCUs [to] lead conversations about linguistic, literate, and cultural pluralism within the field . . ." (162). Using Green's work as a framework, Stewart and Stone have put theory into pedagogical practice by creating materials that show how compositionists at HBCUs might lead the way, and engage black thought and language as central foci. Assignments designed with these theories in mind include linguistic literacy autobiographies that interrogate language—especially black language—thereby allowing for opportunities to put the NCTE-CCCC Students' Right to Their Own Language into practice.

Another unique feature about the writing program designed at Huston-Tillotson University is the fact that the program builds in professional development opportunities to support and enhance Afrocentric design. In the next chapter, Stewart and Stone reflect on a summer institute they hosted, sponsored by the United Negro College Fund, where instructors across various HBCUs were brought together to engage writing pedagogy and practices from well-known scholars in rhetoric and composition. The institute featured the work of Staci Perryman-Clark with Afrocentric pedagogy and Students' Right to Their Own Language for first-year writing courses and Asao B. Inoue's work with antiracist writing assessment. Their specific inclusion of professional-development opportunities corresponds directly with Arnetha Ball and Ted Lardner's desire for WPAs to include "extra roles" as professional development opportunities to explore pedagogies that best support black students (Ball and Lardner 179–80). Furthermore, as Ball and Lardner also assert, a feeling of efficacy is essential for educators when engaging pedagogies that support black students: "Teachers can feel efficacious to the extent that the professional space created for them by the intersection of the program goals and personal commitments is marked by expectations that reflect their voices as competent, trained educators" (180). We clearly see the role of efficacy reflected through Huston-Tillotson's programmatic profile as essential to the support and materials designed for their students.

Principle 2: Programmatic assessment measures are designed with black student success in mind.
As editors, we were careful to include contributions and discussions from both HBCUs and PWIs because engaging black perspectives requires the support of allies who teach and administer at PWIs. While many of the contributions and experiences previously discussed focus on PWI WPAs and black WPAs, we now direct attention to how those who administer writing programs at PWIs can support black students not only through the inclusion of Afrocentric pedagogical materials but also in the implementation of writing assessment and programmatic policies. In "The Legal and the Local: Using Disparate Impact Analysis to Understand the Consequence of Writing Assessment," Mya Poe and her coauthors, according to Inoue, "see much of fairness in assessment hinging on whether an assessment has disparate impact, which can be understood through an assessment's methods" (Inoue 8). When speaking of racial differences in outcomes Poe and her coauthors note the

> unintended racial differences in outcomes resulting from facially neutral policies or practices that on the surface seem neutral. Because discrimination flows from the test design, process or use of test scores, rather than from the intent of the test giver, disparate impact analysis focuses on the consequences of specific testing practices. (593)

In *Antiracist Writing Assessment Ecologies: Teaching and Assessing Writing for a Socially Just Future*, Inoue further argues that we cannot eradicate racism from our writing classrooms unless we eradicate our racist assessment practices first (9). As editors seeking contributions from writing programs that reflect a strong commitment to student success, we looked at PWI writing programs who work toward implementing antiracist writing assessment practices that support black student success. This move led us to Western Michigan's first-year writing-intensive program, developed by Jonathan

Bush, Jeanne LaHaie, and Adrienne Redding.

As the WPA at Western Michigan University, Staci can speak intimately to the institutional context surrounding this program, a program that enrolls between 2,000 and 2,500 students each year. ENGL 1050 is the single largest course at WMU. Data gathered from her institution's Gardner Institute Database revealed that while the failure rate for white students enrolled in ENGL 1050 was 18 percent, the failure rate for black students was 22 percent. Staci, Adrienne, Jeanne, and Jonathon have each written extensively about the ENGL 1050 Intensive program and the theoretical rationale surrounding its pedagogical and administrative approaches (Perryman-Clark, "Who We Are(n't) Assessing"; Perryman-Clark, "Creating a United Front"; Redding, LaHaie, and Bush, "One-on-One"); however, as editors, we believe it is necessary to highlight the ways that it designed explicit assessment approaches and materials to overcome racial disparities among those who successfully pass the course. With this model, the emphasis aligns passing the course with students' abilities to demonstrate proficiency in first-year writing program outcomes by using a one-on-one course format for learning. In their program profile, Redding, LaHaie, and Bush discuss two specific cases, Sherman and Shana, both of whom are African American. While both students were written off by their previous instructors as being unable to pass the course, both were able to succeed and pass the course with a different format. Furthermore, the success of the ENGL 1050 Intensive program has contributed significantly to the overall university retention rate from the first to the second year by increasing this rate to approximately 79 percent. Because roughly two-thirds of the ENGL 1050 Intensive students are members of racial minorities, the contributions from this specific program reveal what first-year writing programs can do to ensure that all students succeed.

Principle 3: Successful writing programs understand that they can implement Afrocentric pedagogy and antiracist writing assessment practices and still support all students.

The ENGL 1050 Intensive program provides us with one practical example of how we can address racial disparities and still support all students: It is a program designed at a PWI institution, where a third of students enrolled in ENGL 1050 Intensive are white, therefore suggesting that engaging black perspectives in writing programs does indeed support and improve retention and learning for all students. Many sources in composition have also written extensively concerning how Afrocentric pedagogy supports all students (see, for example, Richardson, *African American Literacies;* Perryman-Clark, *Afrocentric Teacher-Research*), and Staci has also written extensively about an Afrocentric curriculum designed for a first-year writing course at a PWI (*Afrocentric Teacher-Research*), and shown that these curricula can help students meet the learning outcomes of campus writing programs (Perryman-Clark, "Toward a Pedagogy"). Therefore, we believe that the materials designed by HBCU contributors and offered on our webspace will also be of value for those who administer writing programs at PWIs.

For instance, let's consider Lockett's materials, including her contributions to the revision of their first-year composition student learning outcomes (SLOs). These outcomes include the following, as they move students toward twenty-first-century literacies and new media. Students in the program

- Formulate and craft personal and professional goals for improving their writing
- Develop arguments through a structured revision process that demonstrates a substantial revision (e.g., strengthens the existing genre and/or appeals to various configurations of audiences, purposes, genres, mediums of delivery, and styles)
- Investigate, identify, and compose (rhetorical and literary) characteristics of academic discourse and texts
- Compose and deliver a multimodal composition that strategically uses oral and visual arguments
- Identify, select, evaluate, and (effectively) utilize a range of sources that are integrated into at least one major assignment
- Compose fundamental components of a multipage *persuasive, academic* argument, which expresses the strategic invention and arrangement of claims, reasons, and evidence that

includes considerations of counterargument and ethical use of sources.

- Participate actively in the editorial process with peers, instructors, and the writing center to practice improving the delivery of arguments, in terms of grammar and mechanics (e.g., syntax, diction, punctuation, spelling, and citation), as well as document design.

When including Afrocentric pedagogical materials, Lockett's contribution shows us that Afrocentric materials can still meet the learning objectives designated for a writing program. What is also important to note is how these learning objectives can be applied to any student and not just black students, though the institutional context surrounding the work of HBCUs is distinctive. Finally, it is worth noting how HBCU programs can serve as models that can be included in CWPA assessment galleries that provide models and profiles of institutional writing programs. In short, HBCU models are also useful spaces for helping PWIs transform their writing programs, and we can learn tremendously from the contributions of these programs.

CONCLUSION

In essence, we argue that an essential principle for engaging black perspectives in WPA work is including Afrocentric pedagogical materials, HBCU writing programs, and assessment practices that target black student success. Such a principle can not only improve student learning but also support all students and WPAs who teach at both HBCUs and PWIs. We therefore propose that organizations like CWPA and CCCC more actively include Afrocentric pedagogical and assessment materials in their galleries and revise frameworks for success in postsecondary writing to include and engage black perspectives. In the next chapter, contributors to these institutional profiles will reflect on their curricular designs in relation to black students' success. We also invite readers to visit our webspace, which includes a gallery of resources from these program profiles that engage black perspectives.

WORKS CITED

Asante, Molefi Kete. "The Afrocentric Idea in Education." *The Journal of Negro Education,* vol. 60, no. 2, Spring 1991, pp. 170–80.

Ball, Arnetha F., and Ted Lardner. *African American Literacies Unleashed: Vernacular English and the Composition Classroom.* Southern Illinois UP, 2005.

Council of Writing Program Administrators, National Council of Teachers of English, and National Writing Project. "Framework for Success in Postsecondary Writing." Council of Writing Program Administrators, Jan. 2011, wpacouncil.org/framework.

Green, David F., Jr. "Raising Game." *Composition Studies,* vol. 44, no. 2, Fall 2016, pp. 162–66.

Inoue, Asao B. *Antiracist Writing Assessment Ecologies: Teaching and Assessing Writing for a Socially Just Future.* WAC Clearinghouse and Parlor Press, 2015.

National Council of Teachers of English and Council of Writing Program Administrators. "NCTE-WPA White Paper on Writing Assessment in Colleges and Universities." Council of Writing Program Administrators, http://wpacouncil.org/whitepaper.

Perryman-Clark, Staci M. *Afrocentric Teacher-Research: Rethinking Appropriateness and Inclusion.* Peter Lang, 2013.

———. "Creating a United Front: A Writing Program Administrator's Institutional Investment in Language Rights for Composition Students." *Academic and Professional Writing in an Age of Accountability,* edited by Shirley Wilson Logan and Wayne H. Slater, Southern Illinois UP, 2018, pp. 168–85.

———. "Toward a Pedagogy of Linguistic Diversity: Understanding African American Linguistic Practices and Programmatic Learning Goals." *Teaching English in the Two Year College,* vol. 39, no. 3, Mar. 2012, pp. 230–46.

———. "Who We Are(n't) Assessing: Racializing Language and Writing Assessment in Writing Program Administration." *College English,* vol. 79, no. 2, Nov. 2016, pp. 206–11.

Poe, Mya, Norbert Elliot, John Aloysius Cogan Jr., and Tito G. Nurudeen Jr. "The Legal and the Local: Using Disparate Impact

Analysis to Understand the Consequences of Writing Assessment." *College Composition and Communication*, vol. 65, no. 4, June 2014, pp. 588–611.

Redding, Adrienne, Jeanne LaHaie, and Jonathan Bush. "One-on-One 'Intensive' Instruction: Faculty and Students Partnering for Success in First-Year Writing," *Language Arts Journal of Michigan*, vol. 32, no. 1, 2016, pp. 18–24.

Richardson, Elaine. *African American Literacies*. Routledge, 2003.

Students' Right to Their Own Language. National Council of Teachers of English and Conference on College Composition and Communication, 1974, 2014, http://cccc.ncte.org/cccc/resources/positions/srtolsummary.

WPA Task Force on Internationalization. "Final Report." *Council of Writing Program Administrators*, Mar. 2008, wpacouncil.org/node/1393.

6

Reflective Moments: Showcasing University Writing Program Models for Black Student Success

Alexandria Lockett, Shawanda Stewart, Brian J. Stone, Adrienne Redding, Jonathan Bush, Jeanne LaHaie, Staci M. Perryman-Clark, and Collin Lamont Craig

BUILDING FROM THE FRAMEWORK FOR SUCCESSFUL writing programs in the previous chapter, Chapter 6 provides critical reflections from faculty and instructors teaching at Spelman College, Huston-Tillotson University, and Western Michigan University. Together, we honor the voices of faculty working at HBCUs and allies working at PWIs in the showcasing of African American student work. We frame their reflective insights into challenges and successes as a part of a collective discourse that provides a nuanced and extensive conversation beyond the boundaries of our traditional conversations on WPA work as a practice, place, and identity. We choose to provide critical reflections of each of our voices in this chapter to emphasize the ways in which teachers and scholars may work collaboratively to support black student-writers, model anti-racist assessment practices, and treat race and gender as meaningful frameworks for program development. In previous chapters, each author has called for the inclusion of voices that have traditionally been silenced in WPA narratives.

In this chapter we wish to emphasize common threads of programming that exist across the reflections from these three chosen institutions. These include (1) an attention to and emphasis on black labor and black bodies, (2) an emphasis on curriculum development and assessment practices, and (3) an emphasis on institutional power dynamics, influence, and decision making. Featured materials, sample syllabi, and assignments appear in the online resources associated with this book, found at black-perspectives-in-WPA-resources.ncte.org.

CRITICAL REFLECTION ON SPELMAN COLLEGE:
ALEXANDRIA LOCKETT

Institutional Profile and Program Description

Spelman College, a historically black private women's college, features numerous structural ways for students to engage in the study, teaching, and production of writing, rhetoric, and communication. For example, all Spelman students must satisfy a writing proficiency requirement as part of their general core curriculum. This requirement consists of three components. First, students must successfully complete one semester of First-Year Composition (English 103) or Honors Composition (English 193). Next, they must submit any of their first-year writing (e.g., a researched argument) to a portfolio that is reviewed by an interdisciplinary jury of faculty. Third, they are required to complete writing-intensive (WI) courses in their major.

First-Year Writing at Spelman

Although the Spelman English Department staffs English 103/193 and has the power to determine its student learning outcomes, other administrative units also directly affect how the first-year writing requirement functions. For example, the Office of Undergraduate Studies coordinates each student's first-year experience (FYE), which regulates student registration. All students are required to take first-year composition during their FYEs. Students cannot test out of the course with IB or AP credit. In addition, the honors program director advises honors students and may choose to work with the Honors Composition (English 193) faculty to adapt their course to the rigor of honors student requirements.

Furthermore, students are required to take a unique course entitled African Diaspora and the World (ADW), which decentralizes Eurocentric educational approaches by introducing students to the study of black art, language, and culture all over the world. This course has traditionally relied on English 103/193 to prepare students to read, write, and research in ways that encourage them to perceive themselves as part of an international community of black global citizens. In fact, some instructors who teach English Composition also teach for the ADW program and FYE. That said, the connections between ADW and English 193 could be stronger with regard to scope and sequence.

Program Outlook

Currently, Spelman College is undergoing several leadership transitions that may dramatically alter its writing programs within the next few years. As of 2017, the college has recently hired a new president and provost. Meanwhile, the English Department is undergoing major changes, as well. Since 2014, we have had a total of four retirements, and the departure of three full-time faculty—two senior faculty and one lecturer—which included both the last department chair and the one and only tenured rhetoric and composition faculty member. However, more rhetoric and composition faculty are part of the English Department than ever before. In 2017, we elected a new department chair, and some tenured English faculty are also directing other major programs at the college such as the Comprehensive Writing Program (CWP), the Honors Program, and African Diaspora and the World (ADW). These major administrative and departmental changes will likely affect the curricular design of first-year writing at Spelman, in terms of its staffing, operations, faculty development, and overall support for student and faculty ability to abide by the college's policies and broader strategic planning objectives.

However, the current state of WPA at Spelman also presents certain administrative challenges that are unlikely to change in the near future. At Spelman, the CWP is not an independent administrative unit and there is no official first-year writing program. Since the Writing Center subsumes a major part of its operations, the CWP is frequently confused with being a "writing center" only. This attitude may have contributed to the college's decision to recognize the CWP as part of the Office of Undergraduate Studies' Center for Academic Planning and Success (the CAPS program). On one hand, this administrative location constrains the director's access to funding, which is further complicated by other temporary sources of funding the CWP relies on—namely federal Title III monies. On the other hand, it opens up the potential for WPAs to play a much greater role in assessment at the college.

For example, an initiative such as SpelFolio could move from its current pass/fail model to a longitudinal evaluation of a student's writing development throughout the entire writing proficiency requirement: from the first and second year core courses to advanced major writing-intensive courses. Indeed, the CWP administers SpelFolio, which is a part of the first-year writing requirement. However, faculty receive little or no follow-up communication about the results of SpelFolio and its relevance to how writing and diasporic black literacy is taught. For example, SpelFolio could ask for more reflective writing prompts that directly engage student's understanding of the relationship between ADW and FYC and their personal experiences with these courses. These prompts might ask students to write about multilingualism in the diaspora, language policy, black cultural expression, and community literacy. By scaffolding this kind of assessment, WPAs would generate valuable institutional data about black women's attitudes toward black language learning. This information could help instructors and administrators better understand the kinds of risks students take when communicating about identity and culture.

Another major issue is that first-year writing at Spelman does not have a stand-alone program. This absence may be rooted in a herstory of writing-intensive Afrocentric courses like ADW. A couple of decades ago, Spelman required students to take two—not just one—first-year writing courses alongside two semesters of ADW courses. As previously mentioned, ADW introduces students to a decolonial black perspective on culture and history that destabilizes white-supremacist ideologies of knowledge production. Since many first-year writing faculty teach both types of classes, they have traditionally included strong writing-intensive components. Moreover, their writing courses have often focused on race, racism, and issues of citizenship as they specifically affect black language learners.

The Future of Writing at Spelman: A Reflection

Spelman has the potential to cultivate and demonstrate one of the most powerful examples of an intersectional, transdisciplinary decolonial emancipatory writing culture. If our writing pedagogy truly puts black women's needs at the center of its aims, we will be forced to reckon with the creative limitations of any teaching and learning strategy that only superficially engages matters of race and gender. The struggle to be recognized as worth being seen and heard is a matter of survival intensely experienced by the majority of black women. To illustrate, black women's participation in the acts of reading, writing, and speaking in America is culturally significant because contact with these arts was systematically denied to them during over four hundred years of slavery and reconstruction. In fact, the very existence of black women writers challenges the legitimacy of Western philosophical, legal, and scientific perspectives about the human use of human beings, as it relates to the social construction of race, class, gender, and sexuality.

Through my own first-year and advanced writing courses, I decided to leverage emerging technologies to change the way we tell stories and make facts about black women by organizing a Black Women's Herstory Wikipedia Edit-a-Thon to rectify Wikipedia's lack of coverage about black women in the arts, advocacy, and media. The event was coordinated with Art + Feminism, a distributed global effort that takes place at various locations during March each year. This was the first time that Spelman participated in Art + Feminism, and over a hundred students representing both Spelman and Morehouse, its affiliated men's college, attended this event and learned how to contribute their rhetoric and writing skills to one of the Internet's largest, most popular sites of knowledge making. This event brought many intra-institutional units into contact such as the Honors Program, ADW, the CWP, the English Department, the Bonner Office of Civic Engagement, and the Women's Research and Resource Center, as well as other local institutions like Morehouse, Agnes Scott College, and Emory University.

The Bonner Office recognized the social impact of this public digital writing effort and gave students permission to obtain service hours for participating in the event. This campus recognition of writing was the first of its kind, in the sense that the college embraced a radical womanist online writing event, linking it to writing and research in courses across disciplines and classifications. Furthermore, the event was inextricably connected to prior faculty development initiatives in writing pedagogy. In June 2016, a Morehouse colleague and I had obtained an Associated Colleges of the South Faculty Grant to organize a cross-institutional, interdisciplinary three-day symposium to teach faculty how to integrate Wikipedia into their writing-intensive courses. Thus, a strong groundwork has been established for future WPAs at Spelman, or other HBCUs, to synchronize their interest in representing black culture with teaching writing with dynamic, collaborative technologies.

Overall, I am committed to a vision of WPA at Spelman that seeks to draw on a long tradition of increasing black women's freedom to learn and practice knowledge production through systematic practices of rhetoric, writing, reading, research, and communication with global communities and technologies. This vision sponsors literacies that resist oversimplification, engage complexity, confront uncertainty, and disclose fear of disclosure itself. Emotional costs and benefits of exclusion/inclusion would guide our pedagogy, as we would openly acknowledge insecurity as it manifests itself through our unique individual relationships to feelings of unattractiveness, loneliness, pain, and/or guilt. Such engagement could generate a significant source of creative and critical substance that nurtures the intellectual life of the college.

CRITICAL REFLECTION ON HUSTON-TILLOTSON UNIVERSITY: SHAWANDA STEWART AND BRIAN STONE

Institutional Profile and Program Description

Huston-Tillotson University (HT), located in Austin, Texas, is a private liberal arts university with a student population of about one thousand. Though the university is oftentimes mistakenly identified as having been founded in response to freed slaves being denied admission to other universities in Austin, the truth is that Huston-Tillotson, chartered in 1877 as Tillotson Collegiate and Normal Institute ("Huston-Tillotson University History"), is the oldest institution of higher education in Austin. In spring 2015, we received a grant from UNCF/Mellon Programs to host a teaching and learning institute for English faculty from other historically black colleges and universities across the nation. Our institute, entitled "Centering Students in the First-year Composition Classroom: Engagement, Improvement, and Pedagogical Practices," sought to provide a forum for advanced instruction in pedagogy, research, and assessment for first-year composition faculty at other UNCF/ Mellon member schools.

From our personal teaching experiences, we recognized the divergent beliefs among students, faculty, and administrators at our own HBCU regarding the role of standard edited American written English (SEAWE) in composition classrooms. Due to the perceived importance of such traditional grammatical instruction at our own institution, especially among faculty outside of English, we wanted to further explore the ways writing pedagogies at other private HBCUs were similar to or different from our own and to better understand the extent to which current research in students' rights to their own language and antiracist writing assessment inform the practices of writing instructors at HBCUs. Heeding David F. Green Jr.'s call for "compositionists at HBCUs [to] lead conversations about linguistic, literate, and cultural pluralism within the field of composition" (162), we acknowledge that it is difficult to turn a blind eye to the social and political implications of composition pedagogy that privileges SEAWE and penalizes students for expressing themselves in their home languages. This privileging of pedagogies and assessments designed according to the social and cultural realities of a largely middle-class, white student body has hindered the academic success of African American students for decades (Rickford 1999; Alim 2007) and has not only misrepresented the truth about African American students' academic capacities but has remained a major factor in African American students' academic (un)interest and (un)success.

Accordingly, it is not uncommon to read disparaging statistics about African American student literacy underachievement on national assessments. For instance, the National Center for Education Statistics reports that only 16 percent (the lowest rate of all racial/ethnic groups listed) of African American twelfth graders scored at or above proficient on the reading portion of the 2013 National Assessment of Educational Progress. They also report that the critical reading and writing SAT scores of African American students ranked lowest by racial/ethnic group and below the national average. This account of African American underachievement (and the countless tales of others like it) paints a picture of inability—a "reality" that simply is not true—and these false assumptions risk affecting instructors' attitudes, teaching practices, and philosophies in composition classrooms. In *Critical Race Theory Matters: Education and Ideology,* Margaret Zamudio and her coauthors identify such narratives as the myth of meritocracy. They explain that this myth assumes a level playing field for all students; however, this simply is not the case. Consequently, rather than scrutinize the decisions and structures of educational systems when white students continually *appear* to outperform students of color, the myth of meritocracy assumes that this academic disparity is based on "an individual's efforts and talents" (12) rather than on systemic practices. Zamudio et al. further explain that "the notion of meritocracy is a master narrative that guides our understanding about society in general" (12). As a result, we believe that the work of first-year writing instructors at HBCUs, our students' successes, and the increased publication of both can play a palpable role in dismantling this master narrative.

UNCF/Mellon Institute: A Reflection

In this light, we wanted to provide a space where writing faculty could share their teaching experiences, pedagogy, and writing assessments while also engaging in dialogue with institutional presenters. Drawing from the fields of sociolinguistics, rhetoric, and composition, we offered a four-day, hands-on, interdisciplinary institute where faculty learned, shared, and created composition pedagogy and assessments designed to improve African American student success in first-year composition. We had four presenters— Staci Perryman-Clark, Asao B. Inoue, Brian Stone, and Shawanda Stewart—who each focused on a different component of student engagement, improvement, and pedagogical practice in first-year composition.

On the first day of the institute, Staci Perryman-Clark from Western Michigan University presented "Aligning Students' Right to Their Own Language (SRTOL) with Your Writing Program." During her presentation, Perryman-Clark defined and discussed the sometimes controversial SRTOL, a presentation that initiated meaningful and thoughtful discussion that continued for the remainder of the institute. On Day 2, Huston-Tillotson professors Brian Stone (who now teaches at California State Polytechnic University) and Shawanda Stewart presented "Critical Hip-Hop Rhetoric Pedagogy," a pilot empirical study to investigate students' engagement in a first-year writing curriculum design inspired by the research of H. Samy Alim. On the third day, Asao B. Inoue, Director of University Writing and the Writing Center at the University of Washington Tacoma, defined racist writing assessment and suggested ideas for enacting antiracist writing assessment ecologies in our composition courses. On the final day of the institute, each participant presented for fifteen minutes. Some presented changes they were going to make to already created assignments while others created completely new assignments in response to what we had discussed during the institute.

Discussion and assignment-sharing among institute participants confirmed our attention to Afrocentric education at our HBCUs in part as a result of instructors' purposeful intention to practice pedagogy "grounded in worldviews employing educational practices that are culturally situated within the interests of the people of the African Diaspora" (Perryman-Clark 9), but also because doing so is in large part a unique characteristic shared among our colleges and universities. In arguing for the contemporary necessity of HBCUs, former North Carolina Central University Chancellor Charlie Nelms says: "HBCUs provide a culturally affirming, psychologically supportive environment. Students don't have to prove they belong here" (qtd. in Goode par. 2). At the institute, it became apparent that providing culturally relevant writing instruction is woven throughout our pedagogy because it is not only what we do, but it is also who we are. Despite consensus for the need for and benefits of culturally affirming pedagogy in first-year writing, however, there was a general resistance to a movement away from the need for standard written English as a first-year writing outcome, primarily out of concern over existing social prejudices and campus administrative constraints. Even though institute participants are proponents of pedagogies that resist institutionalized racism and white supremacy and are aware of research that speaks to the benefits of students' rights to their own language, the question remained whether an expectation that students demonstrate a strong command of standard written English in first-year composition is actually a tool to resist institutional racism or one that complies with it.

A UNCF/Mellon Institute Participant's Reflection: James Eubanks, Stillman College

One of the key ideals that I took away from the UNCF/Mellon Teaching and Learning Institute was the need to innovate even in the face of institutional issues. Because of the system in place that governs issues like the number and types of essays that can be assigned at my institution (Stillman College), sweeping pedagogical changes are difficult to implement, especially as I would desire for some of those changes to be rooted in a discussion about student's right to their own language, when much of our instructional aim is to maneuver students toward more standardized communication. So I focused my course adjustments on one unit: argumentation. It is a stated aim in our department to develop more incisively critical thinkers, and learning how to construct and deconstruct argumentation is a crucial part of that development.

I gave students a choice of topics for the main essay, but did not for the reflection that they wrote about the process of argumentation. My thinking behind this change was that in the reflection students would have a low-stakes chance to consider the topic that they could expand on in their essays, if they chose. It is a very nuanced topic and one many students had not considered before, so I did not wish to stake their success solely on their ability to argue well for one side of the issue within the context of written discourse. In classroom discussion, I felt the discussion of students' rights to their own language was a good jumping-off point to begin our discussions of the workings of argumentation and felt that, in the aggregate, the students were engaged and willing to debate one another, as their viewpoints were far more varied than is typically the case if the topic is something they find to be more orthodox, which was something that I found to be true of the discussion we had on the topic at the institute.

All in all, I have been encouraged by my early implementation of strategies that I developed at the institute and will be actively looking for more places in my curriculum where I can implement additional pedagogical strategies based on what I learned.

CRITICAL REFLECTION ON WESTERN MICHIGAN UNIVERSITY: ADRIENNE REDDING, JONATHAN BUSH, AND JEANNE LAHAIE

Institutional Profile and Program Description

Western Michigan University is a public national research university in Kalamazoo, Michigan, established in 1903, with a population of 24,000 students. As WMU's website emphasizes, "[a] wide range of resources and services focus on academic and career success, with several dedicated to meeting the special needs of such select groups as first-year students, transfer students, military veterans and youths who have aged out of the foster care system."

In keeping with the university's prioritizing of student success, the ENGL-1050 [First-Year Writing] Intensive course (1050 Intensive) works in conjunction with the current FYW program, facilitating student success through close faculty engagement with struggling students, as opposed to primarily administratively staffed student-intervention programs. The 1050 Intensive course began in 2014 as an ad hoc attempt to assist students in jeopardy of failing WMU's first-year writing course. We knew from our own institutional data that failing (or receiving a noncreditable grade—below C) was a major marker of loss and retention failure among our first-year students.

It is our contention that composition studies is well-positioned to be a powerful force in retention and success discussions for first-year students. Our experiences and the data already generated by these first six semesters of offering the intensive course as a support to struggling FYW students appear to support that contention. We agree with Pegeen Reichert Powell, who states, "What first-year writing faculty do as a matter of course—teach smaller classes, conduct personal conferences, assign papers that call for personal writing—is a tremendous resource, deliberately or not, for retention efforts and their institutions" (43). And many years ago, Don Murray stressed how even in traditional settings, first-year writing is a place where connections and partnerships, both between instructor and student and between student and student, occur:

> We have to respect the student. . . . We must listen carefully for those words that may reveal a truth, that may reveal a voice. We must respect our student for his potential truth and for his potential voice. We are coaches, encouragers, developers, creators of environments in which our students can experience the writing process for themselves. (13)

What we have learned about our students goes beyond their abilities as writers, and centers more frequently on the challenges they face fitting into a classroom and a system that are foreign, intimidating, and/or inaccessible to them, whether for reasons social, emotional, cultural, or familial.

Our program leverages practices of hospitality, the partnerships and activities we do "as a matter of course" (Powell), and positions them as part of a relationship that extends the natural connections that occur in the FYW classroom. Participating faculty members work individually with their students as mentors, but also as partners in a process of critical thinking skills development, time management, organizational efficiency, problem solving, and life navigation, learning each student's needs, weaknesses and strengths, and academic and nonacademic challenges, and then tailoring instruction style and writing focus to those conditions. The student contributes to the creation of the coursework.

ENGL-1050 Intensive is housed within WMU's English Department. At the program's creation in fall 2014, two board-appointed, full-time, term faculty members were hired and tasked with the program's design, creation, and implementation. This move originated in the narrative of a particular student whose inability to succeed in his first-year writing classroom came to a head when his instructor reported him to the FYW director and wanted him removed from class. The instructor's behavior stemmed from youth and inexperience. The student reacted confrontationally and with attitude. Intervention took place when a composition faculty member, in fact serving as chair of the department at that time, decided to work one-on-one with the student. After being given this opportunity, the student expressed a desire to succeed, recognized and admitted his own culpability in the events that had taken place in the classroom, worked to develop and demonstrate his writing proficiency, and, through this unique approach, passed the course. The department chair and the FYW director saw promise in this process and took action. An unexpected budget surplus generated by an absent senior faculty member opened a one-year window to bring on two entry-level term faculty appointees who could run the 1050 Intensive experiment. In fall 2014, the program was launched. The following academic year, both term appointees had their contracts renewed and funded by the College of Arts and Sciences. Prior to the start of the third year, one of the term appointees pursued and attained a tenure-track position at another institution. The one original term appointee continues to manage the program on a year-to-year contract with the assistance of the composition faculty member (the previous chair of the department from the original narrative) and one part-time instructor.

WMU's general education, first-year writing courses serve more than twelve hundred students each academic year. As is the case at many institutions, these courses are taught almost exclusively by part-time or graduate student instructors, potentially leaving those students facing the greatest challenges to instructors with the least resources, especially in the area of time to dedicate to student needs above and beyond the most basic, in-class matters. Although the English Department cannot radically redesign this system to make full-time faculty the teachers of record in all of these classrooms, it can address this weakness by providing a program like ours to make faculty available to the students in greatest need.

Our statistics reflect that between 18 percent and 22 percent of first-year writing students are not earning the C grade required by most majors. As we enter the sixth semester of running our program, we can say with confidence that many, if not most, of these students are failing for reasons unrelated to academic ability, while a small number require remediation. When designing the program, our goal was to find a time to intervene with these students after warning signals appeared, but before it was too late for them to develop or demonstrate their proficiency with the material the class covers.

Our current practice strives to begin meeting with the at-risk, first-year writing students by Week 7 or 8 of the fifteen-week semester, allowing for six to seven weeks of faculty-student Intensive teamwork. We ask our first-year writing instructors to share names of students about whom they have concerns by semester Weeks 6 or 7, before midterm grades are due. They are required to inform us about students with issues including but not limited to chronic absence, missing assignments, potential physical/mental health issues, low-proficiency work, etc. We provide information and materials to help instructors effectively select students for, and communicate with students about, this program. Initially, instructors emailed our program a list of their qualifying students or a confirmation that they had no students to recommend. This past semester, in order to minimize the turnaround time between our requesting referrals and instructors' submitting referrals, we began using an online survey program as the method by which instructors submit the names of students experiencing difficulties in their classes. They are asked to select from dropdown menus to categorize the type of challenge each referred student displays. The survey program enables us to organize and analyze these data with greater ease and facility. Using this tool seems to have cut around a week of time off the receipt of the bulk of our instructor referrals.

Once instructors recommend students, these students are contacted via email by a program administrator with a brief introduction to the intensive course and an application. Interested students complete the application and either return the form via email or print it out and bring it to the English Department. We are excited about new plans to also use the survey program for the student-application, preprogram survey process next semester. We are thrilled about the ways in which this will consolidate student data, alleviate potential paperwork chaos, and help us better assess and address student challenges. After receiving submitted student applications, we process them and set up individual meeting times with the applicants. In our experience, around 50 percent of those students offered the opportunity to participate in the intensive program actually submit applications. To date, we have been able to find time to work with every student who has asked to participate.

When new students join the intensive program, a form is filed with our registrar's office that removes them officially from their original class and places them into one of three intensive sections of first-year writing. The class shows on all records simply as a different section of the same course they were in previously. However, instead of going to their original classroom of twenty-two to twenty-three students, they meet one-on-one with a faculty member once each week and meet a second time each week as a student-faculty group to produce work in a supported setting.

Western Michigan University's ENGL 1050 Intensive: A Critical Reflection

As was mentioned earlier, oftentimes students who find themselves in danger of failing the first-year writing class have gotten to this point due to some challenge exacerbated by the time/location/environment of their classroom. Their challenges can be life-related: family in crisis, physical health problems, mental health issues such as anxiety or depressive disorder, work-hour conflicts, etc. Their challenges can be academic: students might be second-language speakers for whom class discussion and activity move too quickly, or students who process information and instruction differently, etc. Both of these challenge categories can be dealt with through our intensive scheduling and setting.

First, participating students, in the initial meeting with their faculty member, choose from the options offered to them a time that they feel they can comfortably appear and focus on work. They sign a contract explaining what the two parties can expect from each other. Days of the week when students may have family or work obligations, or times of the day when students may be more likely to experience scheduling conflicts or may be less productive, can be worked around.

Second, the student meets with the faculty member in that person's office, a space usually designed to feel welcoming, comfortable, relatively private, and somewhat personal. Not only are they not required to expose any personal information before a large audience, but their particular challenges, whether those be "life" or "academic" challenges, can be dealt with privately and purposefully, rather than their needs being one set of many, or never recognized at all. Often, their particular challenges can even become the topics they choose to research and write about. One-on-one contact makes it possible for these challenges to be discovered and acknowledged by the instructor and discussed in a private setting with the student, who can then be guided in research and discovery about related issues for the purpose of generating the writing work required by the course.

For students whose language of nurture may involve a discourse community other than the pejoratively termed *prestige English* or *academic English,* such a learning environment can lessen what may feel like the hostility or condescension of the academic community. Students can feel welcomed rather than threatened or judged. Faculty members can appear more approachable, less alien. As Vincent Tinto reinforces, a "sense of belonging" is one of the three key principles affecting students' abilities to make it all the way to graduation. Almost without exception, the reflective writings of students who have successfully completed intensive sections have included comments about feeling listened to, cared about, encouraged, and connected. Past students often come back to their faculty partner's office for a cup of tea and a chance to talk. Faculty members share themselves and their spaces and student relationships have a chance to become grounded.

In addition to these one-on-one meetings in a faculty member's office, students contract to meet one day each week, usually Friday morning, for a two-hour session in the library for groupwork and instruction. All of the intensive students bring their assignments for that week to the university library, where a section of the first floor study space is reserved for them. This time is for them to produce work. Their faculty members, as well as a number of graduate student assistants, are present to answer questions as they occur or to offer direction in order to help students over the hurdles of getting assignments completed. Students challenged by just sitting down and doing what needs to be done are greatly served by this work time. Holding this work session in the library acquaints students with this important space and demonstrates its benefits as a location for productivity.

As explained earlier, this program began as an ad hoc attempt to deal with students who were facing addressable challenges in their first-year writing classrooms. We had no idea what kind of a response we would get if we offered every student in difficulty a chance to work in an alternative learning environment. We were actually a little scared we might be overrun, both because first-year writing instructors would be overly enthusiastic about getting students out of their classrooms, and because students might see an intensive section as an easy way out of a time-consuming obligation. We found we were mistaken.

Worried that more students would apply than we could work with, we designed our initial referral directions to set instructors up as strict gatekeepers of the program, asking them only to recommend students "mathematically incapable" of passing the course by Week 7 or 8. For that reason, we only had fourteen students apply to the program in fall 2014, despite the fact that over sixty sections of the class were being offered. Our hopes that more students could be served led us to rethink the language we used with instructors leading up to the spring 2015 referral time. At that time we instead asked instructors to recommend students "in danger of" not receiving the required C to pass the class. Instructors were asked to refer any student who seemed challenged. This would allow the faculty running the program to have more responsibility for the student acquisition process and decrease potential stress or pressure individual instructors might feel regarding their selection criteria. As a result, we accepted sixteen students into the spring 2015 intensive course despite the fact that only half the number of sections of FYW were being taught, effectively doubling our participation ratio.

So that first academic year we worked with thirty students. Twenty of these students were nonwhite. Of the thirty, twenty-four students who would otherwise have failed the course passed. Of that twenty-four, eleven students registered and participated in classes the following fall semester, a 36 percent retention rate. Our second year running the program, academic year 2015–16, we experienced much more encouraging results. We worked individually with fifty students, thirty-three of whom were nonwhite (continuing a 66 percent nonwhite participation rate). Of those fifty students, forty-seven ended up passing, increasing our passing percentage from 80 percent to 94 percent. But most exciting is our retention figure from that year. Of the fifty students who participated in the intensive course, thirty-two of them, or 64 percent, were currently registered and taking classes in fall 2016. Our retention rate had increased from 36 percent to 64 percent with the population of students with the highest likelihood of leaving the university, students who would have failed first-year writing. The retention rate for students failing 1050 in general, we discovered after doing some statistical analyses last fall, is normally around 32 percent. We hope to continue seeing these kinds of numbers.

In closing, what we do increases the odds that our students will persist with their degrees and strives to make that degree attainment as time- and cost-effective as possible. The program benefits a wide student demographic, but particularly addresses issues of inequality that exist in black and other minoritized student degree attainment, allowing participants to demonstrate or develop desired program outcomes in ways that can be more purposefully Afrocentric and respectful of student lived experience and day-to-day obstacles through, as detailed in *Afrocentric Teacher-Research: Rethinking Appropriateness and Inclusion*, the implementation of linguistically diverse language policies and pedagogies (Perryman-Clark). We build connections between students and academe by forging student-faculty bonds, framing faculty as accessible allies, and, we hope, increasing future help-seeking behavior, often a level of scaffolding black and minoritized students resist and/or feel is not for them. We've created a course in which students have significant input into the class schedule as well as increased investment and interest in the writing they produce, practicing Powell's kairotic pedagogy by encouraging potentially disenfranchised students to locate productive connections between the work they are asked to do and the hurdles they encounter to their academic participation and performance. Finally, we increase university-wide retention.

New Literacy scholar James Paul Gee theorizes that becoming "literate" in any secondary discourse community, in our particular circumstance the academic or university discourse community, always requires more learning and exposure than can take place in a classroom. An enculturation process must occur for fluency to have a chance, and this enculturation requires more of an "apprenticeship" or mentoring system. Often, underrepresented and minoritized students' primary discourse communities contain less transfer of features from secondary, "dominant" discourse communities such as exist in academia and/or professional environments than do those of the average middle-class student. Gee connects exposure to this transfer of features to success and positive assessment of ability in school. He states, "It is a key device in the creation of a group of elites who appear to demonstrate quick and effortless mastery of dominant secondary Discourses, by 'talent' or 'native ability,' when in fact, they have simply *practiced* aspects of them longer" (15). Since over 65 percent of our intensive-course students come to us from black and other minoritized populations, this mentorship enculturation with faculty aware of these realities serves an additional purpose.

TAKEAWAY 1: BLACK BODIES, BLACK LABOR

As Sherri Craig has argued, black bodies have often been rendered invisible in WPA narratives (17). Moreover, while WPA narratives often address labor conditions associated with WPAs, faculty, instructors, and graduate teaching assistants who do the work of writing program curriculum development, instruction, and assessment, the historical presence of the relationship between labor conditions and black bodies is not considered. Despite the call from Collin and Staci to speak truth about the presence of black bodies and labor ("Troubling the Boundaries"), often in relation to microaggressive actions from white faculty and those in positions of power, authority, and privilege, our collective voices seek to reposition black bodies from the margin of WPA narratives to the center.

Our collective reflections similarly position black bodies as the focus of curricular work and development, in particular. From Alexandria's reflection, we learn that in a standalone program, with no officially designated WPA, Alexandria is provided with the responsibility of doing the bulk of the curriculum development and assessment. This is an important distinction to note here, especially given the fact that WPAs are often assigned these duties, many times with compensation, sometimes without. Nonetheless, without a designated WPA, this work is performed, and it is performed without additional compensation by a black and female body. Such a distinction also calls for the need for intersectionality of WPA experiences and narratives. We are also fortunate to examine the ways in which we have leveraged resources to do much of the work of writing programs beyond institutional limits. Even with grant proposals and funding, it is the work of black bodies who made it possible for faculty (most of whom also black reflect black bodies) to travel and attend the UNCF/Mellon institute at Huston-Tillotson University. The curriculum designing was considered extracurricular labor outside of the contractual duties associated with faculty development and WPA work. Put simply, it was black bodies doing this labor. As a collective, we seek to make this labor visible in disciplinary spaces and scholarship.

TAKEAWAY 2: CURRICULUM DEVELOPMENT AND ASSESSMENT PRACTICES

Previously we've discussed the ways in which black bodies have performed labor in relation to curriculum design. It is also important to consider the roles of both curriculum design and writing assessment and the roles that both play with regard to black students' success. With Shawanda and Brian's inclusion of the critical hip-hop course design of James Eubanks (a UNCF/Mellon institute participant), we see the relationship between culturally relevant pedagogy and the role of African-centered content in curriculum design, a point also emphasized in Alexandria's critical reflection on Spelman's ADW course. However, it is also essential to acknowledge the importance of Afrocentric content and student success at PWIs, like Western Michigan University. From Adrienne, Jonathan, and Jeanne's materials, we can better understand the relationships between curriculum development and writing assessment practices.

From the ENGL 1050 Intensive Program, we learn that the traditional curricular space designated did not enhance student success, especially for black students. Therefore, an alternative curriculum, alternative course format, and different assessment practices needed to be created. Of the curriculum, a portfolio-based design that positioned critical literacies and narrative in relation to research writing tasks enhanced students' participation and performance. Moreover, the one-on-one and collective group hybrid format allowed for each student to receive more attention, motivation, and support as students completed and produced work. Of the writing assessment practices, allowing students the opportunity to earn the C as a summative measure of evidence that students belong at the university, and therefore, must be retained, not only supports black students but all students; moreover, Adrienne, Jonathan and Jeanne's work with ENGL 1050I also underscores the ways in which black student success enhances the whole institution, and can even move an entire institution's retention needle forward statistically. We encourage you to review their binder materials at black-perspectives-in-WPA-resources.ncte.org, where they are framed to make the case for student retention.

TAKEAWAY 3: EMPHASIS ON POWER, AUTHORITY, AND INFLUENCE IN DECISION MAKING

The final takeaway we would like to leave with readers is the role that power, authority, and influence play in decision making. At the time of publication, it is important to note, roughly half of the contributors to this collection are untenured. While one of us was the department chair at the time that one of our programmatic initiatives was developed, all others were untenured at the time of the program's creation. Since then, one of us has moved into a dean's level administrative role, while another has served in a similar role in the past. While a couple of us have been or are currently in WPA roles, as this collection demonstrates stakeholders who occupy the upper echelons of academic administration are necessary to move progress for black students forward.

Exploring power and authority as they influence decision making is vital when doing Afrocentric work. In Alexandria's case, with the absence of a formal WPA who can assist in advocacy work, her curriculum development is done with risk as a junior faculty member sans clear guarantees regarding to what degree this work counts for tenure and promotion. The same can be said for the additional curriculum models developed for this collection. In the latter two examples, from both Huston-Tillotson and Western Michigan University, nearly all who do the curriculum work are untenured except for one faculty member. The risks are also high when we consider enrollment, retention, and recruitment of African American students. With these risks in mind, as collaborators for this collection, we further make a plea that this type of curricular work and scholarship receive appropriate credit in tenure and promotion decisions. As such, we strongly assert that these scholarly contributions are examples of productivity that should be credited for scholarship and research. With regard to WPA work and curriculum development, innovative program creation and curricular development must also count as intellectual work (Roen; Rose and Weiser; Micciche) in both print and multimedia platforms. For this reason, we include reflections of the program profiles in this book, in addition to including a large volume of curriculum resources and materials at black-perspectives-in-WPA-resources.ncte.org.

Finally, power and authority must be considered when providing evidence of teaching and professional competence in tenure and promotion decisions. When faculty put together their tenure cases, they must be able to provide evidence of how their teaching promotes student success and affects historically oppressed populations. Recent movements in higher education seem to echo a case for requiring faculty to provide evidence of multicultural teaching for tenure and promotion (O'Meara and Braskamp), especially as it pertains to student success. Thus, not only must curricular models and reflections count as scholarship, but the support that each curriculum provides for African American students as one of many historically oppressed populations should also factor into tenure and promotion decisions built around teaching. Effecting changes such as these, however, requires power and influence beyond what we as contributors can offer in a single collection. In short, our work is a beginning to this conversation, perhaps one that might add a variety of culturally relevant perspectives in doing WPA work, as well as rethinking curricular approaches to be more culturally sustaining to CCCC tenure and promotion guidelines, but might also extend to the institutional sites where we work. In sum, as contributors, we hope to continue this conversation as a way to position black students' success within a twenty-first century geopolitical environment.

WORKS CITED

Alim, H. Samy. "Critical Hip-Hop Language Pedagogies: Combat, Consciousness, and the Cultural Politics of Communication."

Journal of Language, Identity, and Education, vol. 6, no. 2, 2007, pp. 161–76.

Gee, James Paul. "Literacy, Discourse, and Linguistics: Introduction." *Journal of Education*, vol. 171, no. 1, 1989, 5–17.

Goode, Robin White. "The HBCU Debate: Are Black Colleges and Universities Still Needed?" *Black Enterprise,* 15 Feb. 2011, www.blackenterprise.com/lifestyle/are-hbcus-still-relevant/.

Green, David F., Jr. "Raising Game." *Composition Studies*, vol. 44, no. 2, Fall 2016, pp. 162–66.

"Huston-Tillotson University History." *Huston-Tillotson University,* https://htu.edu/about/history.

Micciche, Laura R. "More Than a Feeling: Disappointment and WPA Work." *College English,* vol. 64, no. 4, 2002, pp. 432–58.

Murray, Donald M. "Teach Writing as a Process Not Product." *The Leaflet,* vol. 71, Nov. 1972, pp. 11–14.

O'Meara, KerryAnn, and Larry Braskamp. "Aligning Faculty Reward Systems and Development to Promote Faculty and Student Growth." *NASPA Journal,* vol. 42, no. 2, Winter 2005, 223–40.

Perryman-Clark, Staci M. *Afrocentric Teacher-Research: Rethinking Appropriateness and Inclusion.* Peter Lang, 2013.

Powell, Pegeen Reichert. "Retention and Writing Instruction: Implications for Access and Pedagogy." *College Composition and Communication,* vol. 60, no. 4, June 2009, pp. 664–82.

Rickford, John R. "Language Diversity and Academic Achievement in the Education of African American Students—An Overview of the Issues." *Making the Connection: Language and Academic Achievement among African American Students,* edited by Carolyn Temple Adger, Donna Christian, and Orlando L. Taylor, Center for Applied Linguistics and Delta Systems, 1999, pp. 1–30.

Roen, Duane H. "Writing Administration as Scholarship and Teaching." *Academic Advancement in Composition Studies: Scholarship, Publication, Promotion, Tenure,* edited by Richard C. Gebhardt and Barbara Genelle Smith Gebhardt, Lawrence Erlbaum, 1997, pp. 43–56.

Rose, Shirley K., and Irwin Weiser. "Introduction: The WPA as Citizen-Educator." *Going Public: What Writing Programs Learn from Engagement,* edited by Rose and Weiser, Utah State UP, 2010, pp. 1–14.

Smitherman, Geneva. *Talkin and Testifyin: The Language of Black America.* 1977. Wayne State UP, 1986.

Tinto, Vincent. "Through the Eyes of Students." *Journal of College Student Retention: Research, Theory and Practice,* vol. 19, no. 3, Nov. 2017, pp. 254–69.

United States, Department of Education, National Center for Education Statistics. "Are the Nation's Twelfth-Graders Making Progress in Mathematics and Reading?" *The Nation's Report Card,* www.nationsreportcard.gov/reading_math_g12_2013/#/.

Zamudio, Margaret M., Caskey Russell, Francisco A. Rios, and Jacqueline L. Bridgeman. *Critical Race Theory Matters: Education and Ideology.* Routledge, 2011.

Afterword

Who Is Served, and Gets Served, in WPA Work?

Asao B. Inoue

I FEEL HONORED TO BE ABLE TO OFFER A FEW WORDS as an after-word to this important collection that initiates a much-needed discussion about black WPA work and positionality, which, as these chapters illustrate and argue in various ways, is always situated in larger histories and contexts of white supremacy and structural racism. In one sense, I feel I am not the right person to write such an afterword, only a surrogate, maybe one scholar of color of a few in the disciplines that make up rhetoric and composition who has WPA and assessment experience. While I grew up in a poor black area of North Las Vegas, and my first language was Black English, I am not African American. I have some skin privilege that my black WPA colleagues do not have, even if that privilege is partial, and has never granted me full insider status. While my ancestors in this nation were imprisoned and robbed of their farms, livelihoods, and possessions, this does not compare to the long history of oppression and subjugation that those of African descent endure to this day.

My ancestors immigrated to the United States, settling first in Hawaii. They were not taken from their homes and brought to this land as slaves. Most important, I feel reticent to step in front of any African American scholar who might be able to speak to this volume's contributions and insights for all WPAs, who I am sure is out there pleading and struggling to be heard. Then again, I want to honor Staci Perryman-Clark and Collin Craig's generous invitation to join them and their contributors in this important work. I am grateful for their invitation and confidence in me. So, I say what follows with a compassionate, reverent, and humble heart, with deep appreciation for this chance.

I wish to start by stating who I envision my audience is in this afterword, since it is important to what I say and how I say things. I speak most directly to white WPAs, and only secondarily to black WPAs and WPAs of color. This is because I feel white WPAs need to hear some things that this collection is saying. White WPAs need to listen more carefully to WPAs of color, and should notice how few there are, how few black WPAs there are, and how this condition of our contemporary moment is a deep and historical problem. If you are a white WPA, you are not used to listening to others—listening to *the* Other—rather you likely are accustomed to others' listening to you. This disposition should be noticed, since it is a whitely disposition. And I speak here in this afterword as a WPA of color who has felt too many times over the years that I was not taken seriously, that I was not heard, and in fact, that I was talked down to, as if I were some child in the midst of grown-ups. So, respectfully, I say to my white WPA readers, be silent, listen compassionately, be extra mindful of your reactions to what those in this collection say, and feel where you are uncomfortable. Those are the places you can grow. Then do something to change the WPA conditions you work in. To my WPA readers of color, particularly black WPAs, I speak to you as a collaborator, in some cases as a coconspirator, and hope that what I offer here gives words to what you likely already know and feel.

In the introduction, when speaking from their own experiences, Perryman-Clark and Craig make an important statement that all WPAs, no matter who they are or what kind of institution they work in, would do well to reflect carefully upon. They say that WPA work, "as an amalgamation of experiences, bodies, labor, policies, rules, departments, and documents, is always and already race work" (9). They offer a list of practices and activities that black WPAs engage in that exemplify this race work, and this work is clearly uneven, meaning white WPAs do not have to engage in such work, while black WPAs must make decisions constantly about it, things such as minimizing white anxiety, choosing to be visible (or not) on campus, addressing microaggressions, and teaching (usually in white contexts). They ask: "[H]ow [are] race and racism . . . circulating in our writing programs"? They continue, "[w]e must consider how the policing of black bodies, black labor, and black intellectual work in our writing programs functions as citations of larger political projects to disenfranchise historically vulnerable and marginalized groups" (11).

It is important to repeat, to underline, Perryman-Clark and Craig's important questions, which should be continually asked by all WPAs. Now really, I'm speaking to white WPAs, since black WPAs don't need to be told to do this. They do this race work and see the ways writing programs that they work in and administer function to disenfranchise black and other marginalized students and teachers all the time—it's hard not to see it, or hear it, or feel it every day. As a WPA of color, I've yet to work in or administer a writing program that didn't have at its core issues of racialization, white language supremacy, and racism as structural in its pedagogies, grading practices, and program assessments, and part of being able to notice such things is, of course, one's historical subject position as nonwhite. When you ain't the subject of any sentence in the WPA work around you, you become acutely aware of how you are the object of such work, or how you get ignored or erased. Being a student of color in college, then grad school, then in the profession provides one with an ongoing practice of reflecting on race—again, it cannot be helped. It is difficult not to when shit is unfair all the time, and the white folks around you seem not to see it, or make elaborate excuses for it at every turn. The problem is always something else, never racism, never white supremacy. Given what we know of our histories and institutions, our critical questions as WPAs should start with the assumption of institutional white supremacy. How is the unfairness or failure or difficulties or absences of blacks in WPA positions and work, in graduate programs, *not* a product of the historical conditions of white supremacy?

Part of the inability of many whites to see, hear, or feel the racism that constitutes WPA work, to be unconvinced that WPA work is social justice and antiracist work, to deny that it is race work at all, is not just due to their not being practiced at seeing, hearing, and feeling race as important to what happens in a writing program. It is not just that most whites do not see, hear, or feel how language work is race work. It is also that the historical narratives around race, racism, and civil rights in the United States have been dictated by what Carol Anderson calls "white rage." In her book of the same name, she shows how historically, from the very beginning, whites in the United States have singularly focused their rage on blacks in order to keep them from having access to literacy, attaining civil rights, getting jobs, owning property, going to college, voting, and more. White rage is often subtle and masked through the status quo, through behaviors, actions, and policies that do not account for the unequal racialized ways that students and teachers are racially constructed in writing programs in hierarchical ways. Carmen Kynard's and David Green's chapters in this volume reveal different ways that white rage is masked as other things. Rage is not always a hooded Klansman burning crosses and yelling the N-word at people. It can be the liberal white WPA holding all students to a standard of "clear" writing because "that's what is expected of college graduates." White rage can be masked as intolerance to multiple, and tacitly racialized, ways of communicating in classroom or program. It can manifest itself as annoyance, or disappointment, or an unwillingness to accept other ways of languaging. It can be masked in the disapproval of the way a black colleague acts or speaks because she doesn't seem "professional" (read: white).

One particularly virulent and ongoing manifestation of white rage is the US prison industrial complex, which includes the justice and bail systems (and de facto the black public school system). Michelle Alexander's *The New Jim Crow: Mass Incarceration in the Age of Colorblindness* provides an insightful and well-researched account of how the United States has fashioned its prison system into one that now creates conditions in which more blacks today are brutalized, terrorized, criminalized, and disenfranchised than the total number of black slaves at the end of the Civil War. How does this happen in the so-called "land of the free"? How is it connected to WPAs and their work? It happens because it has always happened—

it's status quo and is framed by the white imaginary as nonracial, and what people deserve. It is connected to WPA because all societal systems, from education to incarceration, are interconnected and they work from interconnected logics and policies that have over the last thirty or so years formalized and legitimized what sociologist Eduardo Bonilla-Silva calls the "new racism" ("New Racism" and *Racism without Racists*; see also Villanueva), which really ain't all that new. A racism that does not need to mention race, but is a metonymy for it. We can speak of language "standards" with no reference to race, but language and any standard is a reference to race because people are racialized in our society and language is only used among groups of people who are racialized—that's why we have such racial and ethnic segregation in where people live today. Economics is another racialized reference, as are "underprivileged" and "urban." All these references have been constructed historically to hide white supremacy and privileges. They are part of the smoke that obscures the mirrors that reflect back toward one another.

The race work of WPA work and literacy classrooms more generally are, of course, connected intimately with the history of the United States. I find Ibram Kendi's history of racism as a set of ideas a good start, as well as Alexander's work mentioned already. Kendi shows clearly the way white people in the United States have used a number of logics, policies, and ideas that can facially seem not to be about race, but of course the intentions and consequences are always to keep the racial hierarchy in the United States the same, maintaining a system of white privileges that are treated as unquestioned white rights. Kendi explains in *Stamped from the Beginning: The Definitive History of Racist Ideas in America* that racism as a set of ideas is persistent and has always been a part of the United States and its common sense and logics. It is this kind of racist history and historical racist common sense in US society and writing programs that creates the kind of white psychology that is prevalent today, a psychology that Robin DiAngelo identifies as "white fragility."

White rage and white fragility are reactive logics that are common in writing programs, even ones run by well-intentioned, liberal white WPAs. Being woke as a white WPA, as we see in this collection's chapters, just ain't enough. This is not to disparage the good ideas of allyship that Scott Wible's chapter suggests, which I read not as old-fashioned notions of white allyship, but of newer conceptions of white coconspirators or accomplices, who tend to focus, as Wible does, on action with and in coordination with people of color, centering people of color and not the white coconspirator. Wible focuses these actions down to a common logic that regulates coconspiratorial actions:

> White allies operate with self-awareness about this privilege and are motivated to put this unearned privilege on the line when they have an opportunity to support and advocate for a person of color—and they don't "just go away when difficulty appears." This ability to effortlessly "go away" when colleagues experience racism comes, of course, from white privilege.

Let me reframe Wible's, Kynard's, and Green's ideas toward ones that I've been most interested in, ones central to all WPA and writing teacher work, ones about assessment. Perryman-Clark and Craig ask initially: "how [are] race and racism . . . circulating in our writing programs"? How are our writing programs "policing . . . black bodies, black labor, and black intellectual work . . . [and] function[ing] as citations of larger political projects to disenfranchise historically vulnerable and marginalized groups"? Of course, my answer is that much policing (but not all) is accomplished through assessment. If Wible's ideas about action-oriented coconspiratorship were actually functioning in a writing program, if those in a program could see, hear, and feel in some way what Kynard and Green articulate about black WPAs and their experiences, regardless of whether that program had the benefit of a black WPA or not, how would classroom grading and assessments be different? How would any articulated standards for writing or communicating be different from what we typically see? How would folks feel about the necessity of the presence of a WPA of color in the program? How would the program serve a black WPA as much as be served by them?

Kynard's chapter is a perfect example of the kind of mandatory reflection that WPA work presents to black WPAs, and that I hear Perryman-Clark and Craig helping us to confront in their questions. Kynard explains the theoretical framework that she uses in her chapter, revealing a good reason for white readers to listen closely, to pay attention to their own fragility as they read this volume, and to understand how important it is for those same readers to understand why feeling good is not an end for antiracist or other social justice work:

> Afro-pessimism gives me the theoretical courage to reject the feel-good performative trends of black scholarship in/for a white academy and critically remind myself that I need not— and, in fact, must not—direct my political inquiry to ready-made solutions that will help white teachers and scholars feel better in a world where black death is routinized. (29)

I find that Kynard also provides black WPAs with courageous words and ways to operate in oppressive white institutions. Afro-pessimism can be used by black WPAs, as Kynard illustrates through her own experiences, not just to survive but perhaps thrive, even change the institution's white status quo. She reminds me that most good changes in history happen through means that do not allow those in control, those who benefit most from the system in place, to feel good, even when they themselves want change. And this insight is perhaps suggested in Kynard's own words. She concludes: "Reconstructing white institutions (or simply accepting more students of color or hiring more faculty and WPAs of color) is not the same as dismantling racial violence." Yes, dismantling racial violence in writing programs will be most painful for the oppressor, for whites, but this does not mean it is bad or unhealthy for them, or for the larger community. In fact, it is quite the opposite.

One area of racial violence I've gestured to but haven't said much about is the assessments of language that WPAs tend to direct or control in some way. I'm speaking of both classroom assessment practices and larger program assessments, such as placement systems and portfolio reading processes that may determine how well a program is meeting the goals or outcomes it has set for itself. While this collection offers several curricular examples in the online resources (black-perspectives-in-WPA-resources.ncte.org), and in Chapter 5 Perryman-Clark and Craig offer a useful critique of the CWPA "Framework for Success in Postsecondary Writing," and provide their own framework for success in writing that centers on African American materials and considers black students more centrally in assessment measures, I still find it difficult to know how a black WPA will negotiate the pressures of a dominant white standard of language that I think Perryman-Clark and Craig's framework and all the curricula displayed here look to displace. Put simply, how do one's assessment practices and judgments change if one wishes to engage in Afrocentric work? Is this work different for white WPAs?

This is not a critique, mind you. Every program, group of students, collection of teachers, geographic location, and set of structural constraints is different, and one place that the forces of white supremacy and racism nonetheless congeal is language assessment. Perhaps one of the many difficulties in approaching any kind of meaningful, revolutionary change in our assessment practices, whether they be classroom assessment or programmatic, is that they are all grounded in an almost unseen, unheard, and unfelt mechanism: judgment. That is, to make a placement from a reading of an essay, or to offer feedback (or a grade) on a portfolio requires judges to make many microjudgments as they read, then larger judgments that are more obvious to us, like "What grade does this paper get and why?" But how many WPAs, when confronted with such a question, "How shall we grade our students' writing?" lead programmatic investigations of the nature of judgment occurring in the program, including the WPA's own judgment practices and results?

Let's spin this out. Take a portfolio that a writing program might use to do some teacher training and program assessment work together, work that might be overtly race work with language. I'm thinking about some version of Bob Broad's dynamic criteria mapping, an inductive process that helps teachers understand the values they use when reading student writing. Let's say that a group of writing teachers, who will be demographically mostly white and female (if national trends are the norm in this hypothetical program), led by a black WPA, has read and discussed this portfolio, and decided it was an "excellent" portfolio, one perhaps worth a high mark (maybe an A) in any given writing course in the program. Why did or should similar portfolios get that high grade? What judgments make up the larger judgement of an A portfolio in this case, and why are those judgments of language preferred over others? How are we, in this situation, doing what Wible asks us to in his chapter, that is, centering black judgment, black language practices, to make our decisions? Of course, I'm suggesting that this last question is not ever asked. And if it was in this case, because there is a black WPA leading or facilitating, there would most likely be allegations of bias, or of an unfair centering on black language practices that is not appropriate for teaching students how to simply "write clearly or well." The black WPA, these allegations might go, wants to privilege black students by making the program value black English more than white English, although likely the binary would be framed as "clear and appropriate English" versus "unclear and inappropriate English." As I've tried to point out above, this kind of framing is new racist framing. It's how white supremacy maintains itself. What is not asked in these kinds of assessment trainings is: where did our judgements of such a portfolio come from? Who formed those ideas and values? What racialized group tends to be associated with linguistic and discursive dispositions? What models of writing in those teachers' heads are they working from, and what are the racial implications of those models? Remember, language is used only by people. People are racialized into groups. So our judgments of language are racialized already. I'm drawing on the research on racial implicit bias (Greenwald and Krieger; Banaji and Greenwald), as well as the research on how our brains think (Kahneman) and make holistic judgements (Haswell).

When I've led white faculty, as well as faculty of color, through such exercises of judgment, what we find every time is that no one escapes a white racial *habitus* in our judgment practices. This is because it is structured into the academy, its training, and its ways of succeeding (and failing). You cannot get to be in a position to teach writing or administer a writing program if you do not take on to some greater degree the dominant white racial *habitus,* which is more than just language, but also sets of accepted behaviors, actions, dress, dispositions, and judgments that are deemed white—some call them "dominant" but that is just a white racial reference. More new racism.

In other places, I discuss what a white racial *habitus* consists of (*Antiracist;* "Classroom Writing Assessment"), so here I'll just briefly identify four of the dispositions and habits of judgment that make up such a *habitus* and that are often rehearsed in judgements of student writing by everyone, regardless of their racial or gender identification:

- **Unseen, naturalized orientation to the world**—an orientation (or starting point) of one's body in time and space that makes certain things reachable; assumes (or takes as universal) proximities (capabilities to act and do things) that are inherited through one's shared space.
- **Stance of neutrality, objectivity, and apoliticality**—assumes or invokes a voice (and body) or its own discourse as neutral and apolitical, nonracial, which might use some of the other habits to reinforce this neutral and objective stance.
- **Individualized, rational, controlled self**—the person is conceived as an individual who is rational, self-conscious, self-controlled, and determined; conscience guides the individual and sight is the primary way to identify the truth or understanding; social and cultural factors are external constraints to the individual.
- **Clarity, order, and control**—a focus on reason, order, and control; thinking (versus feeling), insight, the rational, order, objective (versus subjective), rigor, clarity, and consistency are all valued highly; thinking/rationality and knowledge are nonpolitical, unraced, and can be objective (from the appendix of "Classroom Writing Assessment").

I offer the above not for deep discussion here, but because I think, once they are articulated any reader, regardless of their racial positioning, can see how their own *habitus* matches up to such dispositions. It's hard to escape such habits of judging language, like a need or valuing of something called "clarity, order, and control" or a "stance of neutrality, objectivity, and apoliticality" as important to "good writing" or "effective writing," or even "critical thinking," which all writing programs, and WPAs, are charged to help students achieve in some fashion. While these habits in judgment are not in and of themselves bad, they become problematic when WPAs do not handle them in programs and curricula as historical dispositions that come from racially white groups of people. This means what we actually read as clear and orderly in texts comes from other whitely readings of texts. The idea of neutrality and objectivity is itself often associated with a white voice, an apolitical position in time and space—apolitical relative to the topic being discussed—yet the social turn in rhetoric and composition has made clear that the center of the field does not accept such notions of language and meaning making.

Perhaps the overarching disposition above, the one that shapes any judgment in a classroom or by a WPA, black or not, is a habit in judgment that assumes an "unseen naturalized orientation to the world." This habit of judgment tends to compare the value of language outside of oneself to an unexamined internal language, which in the academy is a white racial language, the language of those in power; who else is in the position of making judgments on language and articulating them, or bestowing such power on others, even people of color?

My point in this final illustration is a similar point to one that I hear rehearsed in each chapter and contribution of this collection. And it might be summed up in a question that is constantly underneath the details and ideas discussed. Dear reader, whether you are black, white, or brown, if you take away your intentions as a WPA, how does anyone know the ways you frame WPA work and the work that happens within the writing program in which you circulate? What is that framing? What political and racialized allegiances does that framing entail? Whom does it serve most, or primarily, that is, whom does it serve first, then second, etc.? I think the editors and contributors of this collection are arguing that it is about time someone else was served first in WPA work and writing programs.

WORKS CITED

Alexander, Michelle. *The New Jim Crow: Mass Incarceration in the Age of Colorblindness.* New Press, 2012.

Anderson, Carol. *White Rage: The Unspoken Truth of Our Racial Divide.* Bloomsbury Publishing, 2016.

Banaji, Mahzarin R., and Anthony G. Greenwald. *Blindspot: Hidden Biases of Good People.* Delacorte Press, 2013.

Bonilla-Silva, Eduardo. "'New Racism,' Color-Blind Racism, and the Future of Whiteness in America." *White Out: The Continuing Significance of Racism,* edited by Ashley W. Doane and Bonilla-Silva, Routledge, 2003, pp. 271–84.

———. *Racism without Racists: Color-Blind Racism and the Persistence of Racial Inequality in the United States.* Rowman & Littlefield, 2003.

DiAngelo, Robin. "White Fragility." *International Journal of Critical Pedagogy,* vol. 3, no. 3, 2011, pp. 54-70.

Greenwald, Anthony G., and Linda Hamilton Krieger. "Implicit Bias: Scientific Foundations." *California Law Review,* vol. 94, no. 4, July 2006, pp. 945–67.

Haswell, Richard H. "Rubrics, Prototypes, and Exemplars: Categorization Theory and Systems of Writing Placement." *Assessing Writing,* vol.5, no. 2, 1998, pp. 231–68.

Inoue, Asao B. *Antiracist Writing Assessment Ecologies: Teaching and Assessing Writing for a Socially Just Future.* WAC Clearinghouse and Parlor Press, 2015.

———. "Classroom Writing Assessment as an Antiracist Practice: Confronting White Supremacy in the Judgments of Language." *Pedagogy: Critical Approaches to Teaching Literature, Language, Composition, and Culture,* vol. 19, no. 3, 2019, forthcoming.

Kahneman, Daniel. *Thinking, Fast and Slow*. Farrar, Straus and Giroux, 2011.

Kendi, Ibram X. *Stamped from the Beginning: The Definitive History of Racist Ideas in America*. Nation Books, 2016.

Villanueva, Victor. "Blind: Talking about the New Racism." *The Writing Center Journal*, vol. 26, no. 1, 2006, pp. 3–19.

INDEX

Note: An *n* following a page number indicates a note; an *f* indicates a figure.

EDITORS

Staci M. Perryman-Clark is an internationally known scholar who has published widely in rhetoric and writing studies. She is associate dean of the Lee Honors College and associate professor of English at Western Michigan University. Perryman-Clark is the author of *Afrocentric Teacher-Research: Rethinking Appropriateness and Inclusion* (2013); coeditor of *Students' Right to Their Own Language: A Critical Sourcebook* (2014); the 2015 recipient of the WMU College of Arts and Sciences Faculty Achievement Award for Excellence in Research, Scholarship, and Creative Activities; and the 2018 recipient of the College of Arts and Sciences Faculty Achievement Award for Excellence in Diversity and Inclusion.

Collin Lamont Craig is a published scholar in rhetoric, writing, and literacy studies. He is the project coordinator for the Black and Latino Male Initiative at Hunter College and an associate professor at St. John's University. His primary area of scholarship focuses on Black and Latino college male literacy repertoires. He also researches race, gender, and writing program administration. Craig is the author of the forthcoming book, *Lives We Tell, Revolutions We Live: Black and Latino Literacies* (2020).

CONTRIBUTORS

Jonathan Bush is professor of English at Western Michigan University, where he teaches English education, writing, and rhetoric. He has published and presented widely in NCTE journals and other forums. He is a former member of the NCTE Editorial Board and the AP Language and Composition Development Committee, as well as the founding coeditor of *Teaching/Writing: The Journal of Writing Teacher Education*. He currently directs the Third Coast Writing Project and serves as president of the Michigan Council of Teachers of English. He is also a public affairs officer in the Navy Reserve and an Afghanistan veteran.

David F. Green Jr. is director of the Writing Program and assistant professor of English at Howard University. He remains committed to serving historically underrepresented students and theorizing rhetoric and composition practice at minority-serving institutions. He is the editor of *Visions and Cyphers*, a writing studies textbook composed with an emphasis on culture and language research in composition studies, and has published several articles on race, writing, assessment, and critical language use in such journals as *College English, Understanding and Dismantling Privilege, Changing English*, and *Composition Studies*. Green has served as program chair for the 2018 symposium on Teaching Composition and Rhetoric at HBCUs. His research interests include hip-hop, African American rhetoric, critical pedagogy, and emancipatory composition studies.

Asao B. Inoue is professor and associate dean of the College of Integrative Sciences and Arts at Arizona State University, as well as Chair of the 2019 Conference on College Composition and Communication. He is a past member of the CCCC Executive Committee and of the Executive Board of the Council of Writing Program Administrators. Among his many articles and chapters on writing assessment, race, and racism, his article "Theorizing Failure in U.S. Writing Assessments" in *Research in the Teaching of English* won the 2014 CWPA Outstanding Scholarship Award. His *Race and Writing Assessment* (2012, with Mya Poe) won the 2014 NCTE/CCCC Outstanding Book Award for an edited collection, and his *Antiracist Writing Assessment Ecologies: Teaching and Assessing Writing for a Socially Just Future* (2015) won the 2017 NCTE/CCCC Outstanding Book Award for a monograph and the 2015 CWPA Outstanding Book Award. In November of 2016, he guested coedited a special issue of *College English* on writing assessment as social justice. His most recent coedited collection is *Writing Assessment, Social Justice, and the Advancement of Opportunity* (2018, with Mya Poe). His newest book is *Labor-Based Grading Contracts: Building Equity and Inclusion in the Compassionate Writing Classroom* (2019).

Carmen Kynard is associate professor of English and gender studies at John Jay College of Criminal Justice and associate professor of English, urban education, and critical psychology at the Graduate Center of the City University of New York. She interrogates race, Black feminisms, AfroDigital/African American cultures and languages, and the politics of schooling with an emphasis on composition and literacies studies. Her first book, *Vernacular Insurrections: Race, Black Protest, and the New Century in Composition-Literacy Studies,* won the 2015 James Britton Award and makes Black Freedom a twenty-first-century literacy movement. Her current projects focus on young Black women in college, Black Feminist/Afrofuturist digital vernaculars, and AfroDigital Humanities learning. Kynard traces her research and teaching at her website, "Education, Liberation & Black Radical Traditions for the 21st Century" (http://carmenkynard.org).

Jeanne LaHaie teaches first-year composition and literature at Klamath Community College in Southern Oregon, where she is the writing program administrator. She also developed and runs a program to allow students to bypass a level of developmental writing and move directly to the credit-bearing course; these students are successful at higher rates than traditional students.

Alexandria Lockett is assistant professor of English at Spelman College, where she led the First-Year Writing Committee (2014–2017), co-directed the writing-intensive initiative (2015–2018), and organized the institution's first-ever Art+Feminism Wikipedia edit-a-thon (2017). She publishes about the technological politics of race, surveillance, and inclusion in her forthcoming coauthored book, *Race, Rhetoric, and Research Ethics*; in the journals *Composition Studies* and *Enculturation*; as well as in chapters featured in *Out in the Center* (2019) and *Bad Ideas about Writing*. An extended biography is available via her portfolio at www.alexandrialockett.com.

Adrienne Redding is a faculty specialist in the English department at Western Michigan University. She was a creator of and currently directs the English department's First Year Writing Intensive, a retention and persistence program focused on struggling first-year writers. She also serves as a coordinator for the English department's Developmental Writing program. In addition to teaching writing, she regularly teaches linguistics courses such as the Development of Modern English, as well as a Shakespeare Seminar and Western World Literature. Before teaching at WMU, Redding served as a faculty member at Andrews University, where she taught composition, as well as ESL courses at all levels of proficiency; she also supervised the University Writing Center. Her research interests include issues surrounding student persistence and retention, minoritized and marginalized student voices in the first-year writing classroom, and "othered" language and power in both contemporary and Early Modern English cultures.

Shawanda Stewart teaches writing and rhetoric courses in the Department of English at Huston-Tillotson University. Her primary research interests include African American rhetoric, language ideology and culture, and first-year composition pedagogy. Stewart has a genuine interest in research and scholarship that examines and promotes voice and identity authenticity through language in the college composition classroom.

Brian J. Stone is director of Writing Programs and assistant professor of English at Indiana State University (ISU). For more than a decade, he has taught first-year writing at institutions of higher education committed to serving historically underrepresented students. At ISU, Stone has revised the writing program with the goal of developing a socially just first-year writing experience and a culturally sustaining assessment initiative. With Shawanda Brown Stewart, he has authored a number of articles on critical hip-hop rhetoric pedagogy, a culturally sustaining pedagogy, and the first-year writing curriculum developed at Huston-Tillotson University.

Scott Wible is associate professor of English at the University of Maryland, College Park, where he directs the Professional Writing Program and teaches undergraduate and graduate courses in professional writing, design thinking, and composition theory. His research on rhetorical education, public policy, and language diversity has appeared in *College Composition and Communication*, *College English*, *Cultural Studies*, and *Rhetoric Society Quarterly*, and his book *Shaping Language Policy in the U.S.: The Role of Composition Studies* (2013) won the CCCC Advancement of Knowledge Award. Wible is currently at work on a book project that explores the rhetorics, practices, and pedagogies of social innovation in higher education.

Vershawn Ashanti Young is a professor in the Departments of Communication Arts and English Language and Literature at the University of Waterloo, Ontario, Canada. He is perhaps best known for his scholarship on the concept of code-meshing, which promotes writers and speakers using their home linguistic backgrounds to communicate, particularly in high-stakes communication situations. He has authored or coauthored nine books, including *The Routledge Reader of African American Rhetoric* (2018), *Neo-Passing: Performing Identity after Jim Crow* (2018), *Antiracist Pedagogy in Writing, Rhetoric and Communication* (2017), and *Other People's English: Code-Meshing, Code Switching, and African American Literacy* (2018). Young is currently completing the book *Straight Black Queer: Gender Anxiety and the American Dream.*

BOOKS IN THE CCCC STUDIES IN WRITING & RHETORIC SERIES

This book was typeset in Garamond and Frutiger by Barbara Frazier.
Typefaces used on the cover include Garamond and News Gothic.
The book was printed on 50-lb. White Offset paper
by Seaway Printing Company.